Resources for Teaching

ReMix

reading + composing culture

Resources for Teaching

ReMix

reading + composing culture

Catherine G. Latterell
PENN STATE ALTOONA

BEDFORD / ST. MARTIN'S
Boston ◆ New York

For information, write: Bedford/St. Martin's, 75 Arlington Street, Boston, MA 02116
(617-399-4000)

ISBN: 0–312–44476–1
EAN: 978–0–312–44476–1

Instructors who have adopted *ReMix* as a textbook for a course are authorized to
duplicate portions of this manual for their students.

Contents

1 Identity

... or, who do you think you are?

American culture centers on individualism. The Constitution and Bill of Rights, legal decisions, and politics all work together to protect the rights of the individual and promise that every American shall enjoy "life, liberty, and the pursuit of happiness." For more than two centuries, American culture has rested on the central tenet that every person has the right to choose whom he or she is—and can be—regardless of any social status that might be conferred at birth. The American dream itself springs from the idea that people have the power to create and sustain their own identities. But as the readings in this chapter show, individual identities are not easily defined, are strongly influenced by cultural factors, and are not particularly stable once they've taken form.

Identity is a personal topic; as such, it's a natural starting point for a writing class. At the same time, however, students not yet practiced in cultural analysis might resist questioning the personal truths they take for granted. You may, therefore, want to begin your course in less volatile territory and turn to identity at midpoint or later. Your choice will depend on the kind of writing you want your students to produce: If you plan to progress from personal to analytical writing in a composition sequence, beginning with identity makes sense. If your focus is more on sustained critical analysis, identity might be too charged for the first week.

Regardless of at what point you address identity in your course, the Examining the Everyday assignment that opens the chapter offers an ideal way to introduce the topic. For one thing, the project is inherently entertaining: Students are likely to be surprised by at least a few of the items they find in their own wallets and should enjoy trying to puzzle together a picture of themselves based solely on what they carry around with them every day. At the same time, attempting to define themselves will prod students to start questioning how identity is formed. Students may find that the contents of their wallets give a workable sense of who they are, but that simple objective facts and scraps of information are insufficient to fully explain their identities.

Whether they're young adults living away from home for the first time or nontraditional students attempting to fit college into established lives, your students will naturally understand that identity formation is complex and that the self is malleable, since they're likely in the midst of redefining themselves and negotiating multiple influences with their senses of who they are. Before you have them read the chapter introduction, you may want to explore, as a class or as a preliminary journal assignment, what assumptions your students currently hold about their own identities. Brainstorm as a group what "identity" means and what elements contribute to it. Who are your students? What defines them? Why are their identities important? Can they change? This can be a good way to break the ice at the beginning of the term as well.

Because the central assumptions outlined in the chapter's introduction form the basis for analyzing the readings, spend some time discussing them in class. Use the questions that follow each discussion of an assumption to explore the concept with your students. You might want to ask whether your students agree or disagree with the outlined assumptions, as well as what other assumptions about identity they can pinpoint. Discuss with your class, also, how these assumptions function in American culture: Who holds them? What purposes do they serve? Are they helpful or harmful? And how do students see them played out in their personal lives and in the world around them?

All of the readings in this chapter explore one or more of the three main assumptions outlined in the introduction—identity is what we are born with; identity is shaped by culture; identity is shaped by personal choices. Kathy Wilson, Lucy Grealy, and Firoozeh Dumas provide compelling personal accounts that reveal the complexities of identity formation. Gloria Anzaldúa mixes personal experience with cultural criticism to argue that cultural influences on identity are flawed but can be overcome with effort. Michelle Lee's "The Fashion Victim's Ten Commandments" (p. 69) offers a tongue-in-cheek criticism of personal attire that questions how accurately appearance reflects who we are, and Shannon Wheeler's cartoon reveals that dislikes are as significant as likes are in establishing identity. For more analytic studies, you'll find that Emily White's "High School's Secret Life" (p. 15) offers a good model of objective cultural evaluation based on observation; Andrew Sullivan's "The 'He' Hormone" (p. 25) reviews scientific studies to complicate the idea that identity is established by biological factors; and Russell Thornton examines a new option on the 2004 census to argue that cultural definitions of a person's identity are politically more significant than personal choices. Visually oriented students will be especially intrigued by the photobooth snapshots in the Sampling the Old and the New feature on pages 40–41, the images of September 11 memorial tattoos on pages 49–51, and the photo essay on page 12 that explores what a group of 10-year-olds want to be when they grow up.

Additional Resources

Nonfiction

Leslie Zebrowitz, *Reading Faces: Window to the Soul?* (1997)   How much do
our faces reveal about who we are? In this scientific study, Zebrowitz analyzes the facial cues to which humans are most likely to respond.

Fiction

Ralph Ellison, *Invisible Man* (1952)   A seminal work on African American
identity, *Invisible Man* follows its unnamed narrator through a series of
painful realizations about how others perceive him.

Film

Napoleon Dynamite (2004)   In the opening credits of this off-kilter comedy,
articles from the main character's wallet give viewers a first glimpse of his
personality.

Vertigo (1958)   A retired police detective, obsessed with a young woman who
committed suicide, finds both solace and torment in someone who seems
to be her doppelganger.

Web

ID/entity: Portraits in the 21st Century, http://identity.media.mit.edu/
exhibition.html   The portraits featured on this site were exhibited in 2001
at an MIT conference on how technology changes our concept of identity.

Emily White, **High School's Secret Life** (p. 15)

In this excerpt from *Fast Girls: Teenage Tribes and the Myth of the Slut,* Emily
White examines high school cliques to explore external influences on identity
and the effects of personal identity on social interaction. Anybody who has faced
the high school caste system will likely embrace White's analysis and locate him-
or herself on a point of the social spectrum she describes. Although it will be productive for your students to examine their own experiences in the context White
provides, encourage them to question her (and their own) assumptions. Try having students self-identify according to White's classifications: In their experiences, who was a popular kid? Who was a loner? A computer genius? A theater
kid? A natural helper? A rowdy boy? What groups has White left out of her tax-
onomy?

You might begin discussion by asking your students what connotations the
word "tribe" holds for them. White's comparison of teenage cliques to tribes suggests that forming social groups is primitive, instinctual, and not a little violent.
At the same time, it implies that belonging to one of these groups is essential for
survival. Members of a tribe share identity markers and, formally or informally,

ascribe to a set of rules of behavior. This bond gives individual members a sense of who they are. Be aware that some of your students may be bothered by the racial connotations of the word "tribe" and by the absence of students of color in White's population sample. If this issue comes up, encourage your class to explore the racial implications of White's analysis and to consider how her argument might be affected if the students she studied weren't such a homogenous group.

Interrogating Assumptions

Clearly, White believes that cultural factors are the strongest determinant of a student's identity. As she describes it, something as arbitrary as a lunch period assignment can alter Calhoun students' social relationships and their sense of who they are. Although White's observations are compelling, encourage your students to challenge them: How much of what she describes is cause, and how much is effect? That is, are similar students naturally drawn to each other to form groups, or do teenagers reshape themselves to conform to existing groups' expectations? And to what extent do people's physical identity and personal choice determine their eligibility for different groups? Could the overweight girl or the boy with a neurological disorder, for example, ever hope to insinuate themselves into the popular crowd? Does being "physically well proportioned" (par. 11) insulate a student from "loner" status? Can the football quarterback successfully choose to reposition himself as a "theater kid"?

Writing about Cultural Practices

This assignment offers an ideal early writing activity. With its emphasis on focused observation and specific details, it allows students to practice reading culture critically without the pressure of having to formally analyze what they find. Their goal should be to write a descriptive essay that incorporates an abundance of detailed examples from their field observations and that organizes their findings into coherent categories. Students' natural inclination will be to answer each of the assignment's questions in turn; although that can be a useful way to structure an essay, encourage them to let their own ideas determine the shape of their writing. Alternatively, you may want to structure this assignment as a group project in which three or four students observe and verbally report their findings to the class. By hearing each other's examples and categorizations, they will be exposed to the sheer number and variety of details available for inspection and will have an opportunity to consider the different conclusions that can be drawn from similar evidence.

Additional Resources

Nonfiction

Ethan Watters, *Urban Tribes* (2003)   Watters explores tribal behavior among twenty- and thirtysomethings. For these "yet-to-be-marrieds," tribes provide a support system that stands in for the traditional family.

Fiction

Margaret Atwood, *Cat's Eye* (1988)   Atwood's novel of adolescent friendship exposes the casual cruelty that can surface in female relationships.

Film

The Breakfast Club (1985)   A day of forced interaction exposes the artificiality of high school "types": "A brain, and an athlete, and a basket case, a princess, and a criminal."

Mean Girls (2004)   Lindsay Lohan plays an outsider who tries to infiltrate her school's popular clique, the "Plastics."

Television

Freaks and Geeks (1999)   Though it lasted for only one season on network TV, this series (now available on DVD) was celebrated by critics as an honest look at high school life from the perspective of outsiders.

Web

New York Times Multimedia, http://www.nytimes.com/pages/multimedia/index.html   Fred Conrad's "Tribes of New York" series offers introductions to a number of subcultures. Scroll down to "Interactive Features" to see his interviews with goth girls, bike messengers, and baseball fans.

Kathy Wilson, **Dude Looks Like a Lady** (p. 21)

Kathy Wilson's engaging personal narrative presents a surprisingly complex example of identity formation. By insisting that her breasts should trump her hairstyle in how others interpret her femininity (the original title for this piece was "It's the 40 Cs!"), Wilson seems to favor born attributes over choice in establishing her own identity. Despite her unorthodox hairstyle, however, she embraces other cultural markers of femininity: She refers to herself as having "a pretty, round, brown face and dark eyes," is proud of her breasts, and thinks of her short hair as "cute." Students will recognize that Wilson resists cultural impositions on her sense of self, but ask them to consider how other people's assumptions affect her: How do the confusion, condescension, and hostility raised by her appearance influence the way she describes herself?

As the episode in the ice-cream shop illustrates, gender is so central to our sense of identity that misinterpreting it can be cause for severe embarrassment on the part of the person making the mistake, discomfort for the person misidentified, and outrage for a bystander. Wilson's experience reveals that short hair is associated with masculinity and that people notice it before they recognize more fixed aspects of gender, such as breasts or facial characteristics. What is not so immediately apparent is that a woman's refusal to conform to social expectations is itself considered unfeminine. In the bookstore episode, "Redneck Man" interprets Wilson's boyish appearance as license to verbally assault her. To underscore how the element of personal choice affected his response, you might ask your students whether he would have been likely to hurl the same demand at Wilson if she had long hair and a flat chest.

Although she writes that her essay "is about hair, breasts, and identity" (par. 3), Wilson also makes several references to racial issues. She compares her youthful abundance of black hair, for example, to the "flaxen-haired white girls throwing their manes around" (par. 7), concluding that she could never meet cultural preferences for women's hair. As a black woman conducting her business in predominantly white environments, Wilson is very conscious of her race. Although the white people she encounters make no direct reference to her color, she ascribes racial motivations to their behavior: The "silver-haired matron" shows an air of condescension in her outrage; "Redneck Man" reminds Wilson of a schoolmate's implicit threats of lynching. It's worth noting, as well, that the essay makes clear that the black pride and black power movements of the 1960s and '70s contribute to Wilson's sense of who she is; her own cultural traditions give her the strength to shake off her anger and the confidence to keep the personal identity markers she has chosen.

Writing about Cultural Practices

Students may have a hard time choosing a topic for this assignment, which calls for a critical analysis of a narrowly defined subject. You may need to work with the class to brainstorm examples of gender markers in American culture. Remind students that gender is more complex than sex: It includes sexual orientation, for example, as well as the degree of masculinity or femininity a person embraces. Remind them, also, that what may be deemed acceptable in one subculture can put people who don't share that culture on edge. Students may, therefore, want to question what "acceptable" means before they begin writing.

A successful paper will examine a tightly focused cultural marker (a lower-back floral tattoo, for example, as opposed to tattoos in general), consider its meanings for both the person displaying it and the people observing it, and explore the conflicts that arise from differing perspectives. Encourage your students to use Wilson's essay as a model for their own analysis. Personal experience can make for a productive topic, but students must be careful to read an experience critically—not simply narrate it or offer it up as an example.

Additional Resources

Nonfiction

Ayana Byrd and Lori L. Tharps, *Hair Story: Untangling the Roots of Black Hair in America* (2001)   African American hairstyles have meaning beyond the current trends. Byrd and Tharps interrogate the political and social significance of hair.

Naomi Woolf, *The Beauty Myth* (1991)   Woolf's landmark study of physical expectations and their effects on women takes on new meaning in the age of *Extreme Makeover* and *The Swan*.

Susan Bordo, *Unbearable Weight: Feminism, Western Culture, and the Body* (1993)   Bordo's feminist analysis of media includes a section on the advertising pressure on women to mold their bodies to cultural ideals.

Television

Queer Eye for the Straight Guy   This makeover program attempts to improve heterosexual men by endowing them with stereotypically gay traits: style, grooming, and social grace.

Web

After Ellen, http://www.afterellen.com/TV/thelword/butch.html and http://www.afterellen.com/TV/thelword/femininity.html   This site, which focuses on the portrayal of lesbians and bisexual women in the media, presents two views of the TV series *The L Word*. The discussion of how butch or how feminine the women should appear centers on their hairstyles.

Andrew Sullivan, **The "He" Hormone** (p. 25)

Andrew Sullivan is as well known for his conservative politics as he is for being openly gay. Because he backs his argument in this essay with numerous references to scientific studies and to statistics, your students may not recognize right away that Sullivan's argument is controversial and his position deliberately provocative. Point out that he is careful to withhold his thesis until the end of the article: Sullivan argues that because inequality between men and women is caused by biological, not cultural, factors, it should neither surprise nor distress us. His argument hinges, however, on the unstated assumption that high-testosterone traits (such as aggression, competition, and risk taking) are inherently superior to low-testosterone traits (such as introspection, relationship building, and cautiousness). Sullivan does not question why "masculine" behaviors and professions are more valued by American society than "feminine" ones are, but encourage your students to address the issue. What historical and cultural factors has Sullivan excluded from his analysis, and how does that influence the effectiveness of his argument?

By presenting volumes of scientific information before articulating his thesis, Sullivan is employing a tactic often successfully employed by people advancing unpopular arguments. The rhetorical strategy is meant to make the writer's conclusions appear inevitable. Certainly, Sullivan presents evidence that initially appears irrefutable: Throughout his essay he refers to clinical experiments (pars. 12, 28), psychological and sociological studies (17, 19–21, 23), and statistics (10, 24, 30, 32). Although he cautions that many would question the methods used by the researchers he cites (19), he relies on their results to bolster his argument and draws on anecdotal evidence (13, 15–16, 33) and personal experience (1–9, 43) to dismiss any apparent weaknesses of the scientific research.

Many students will be reluctant to question Sullivan's evidence or impugn its objectivity: Because most of it is drawn from scientific studies, students are likely to believe that it is factual and unassailable. You may need to inform them that the question of objectivity (or lack thereof) lies in the author's interpretations of the evidence he presents. Choose a single piece of evidence and ask your students whether they can develop any reasonable interpretations that differ from Sullivan's. Are there other kinds of evidence that could strengthen or weaken his argument?

Interrogating Assumptions

At one level, Sullivan embraces the notion that biology is the strongest determinant of identity. As he sees it, relative levels of testosterone affect everything from appearance to mood to behavior. Variable levels of the hormone affect his self-perception in predictable cycles, and he argues that biology "is at the root of" socialization (par. 3). Because testosterone levels fluctuate, however, and because it's available in a synthetic form that can be easily introduced into the bloodstream, the identities conferred by the hormone are profoundly malleable.

Writing about Cultural Practices

Students who don't consider themselves capable of analyzing written works are often quite adept at reading advertising images critically. This assignment lets students draw on their cultural expertise to gain practice expressing their instinctual analytical skills in writing. Although most students will consider themselves savvy consumers of marketing messages, tell them you expect them to focus on details from the images themselves and to question every aspect of a given advertisement. In addition to men's and women's bodies, for example, students should take a close look at the image's setting and any props or other objects included in the photograph to assess the cultural implications of the visual message.

To help focus their analysis, students should examine the images in the context of Sullivan's argument. Have them look for the typically "masculine" characteristics Sullivan cites as culturally dominant and determine how those characteristics are portrayed by men and women both. Students should also be careful to consider the audience for the advertisements they choose to examine, questioning how the gender, age, and class status of the target market—as well as the nature of the product being advertised—affect the advertiser's manipulation of cultural expectations regarding masculinity and femininity.

Additional Resources

Nonfiction

Gail Bederman, *Manliness and Civilization: A Cultural History of Gender and Race in the United States, 1880–1917* (1995)   This history of gender constructions focuses on the changing formulations of "manliness" and "civilization," examining their effects on figures as varied as Jack Johnson, Charlotte Perkins Gilman, and Theodore Roosevelt.

Fiction

Jeffrey Eugenides, *Middlesex* (2002)   The narrator, Cal, recounts his childhood as a girl, Calliope, and his adolescent discovery that he was born a hermaphrodite.

Television

Sex: Unknown (2001)   This PBS *Nova* documentary about David Reimer, a boy who was raised as a girl after a botched circumcision, is now available on video. You can also view the program's companion website at http://www.pbs.org/wgbh/nova/gender/.

Web

Daily Dish, http://www.andrewsullivan.com   Andrew Sullivan's blog follows developments in politics and current events. Under the "Culture" tab you can read other essays, including "Dumb and Dumber: These days, it's hard to be a man vaguely connected to a brain."

"Sex and Science," http://www.msnbc.msn.com/id/6856839/site/newsweek/   Harvard president Lawrence Summers started a nationwide debate when he suggested that women's brain chemistry might be less suited to math and science than men's. This article from *Newsweek* provides an overview of the controversy and contains audio clips of responses to Summers.

Lucy Grealy, **Masks** (p. 42)

Lucy Grealy, who died in 2002 from a heroin overdose, did not fit in with her childhood schoolmates for several reasons: She was absent for long periods of time, she was from another country, she was sick, and she didn't look like everybody else. This excerpt from her 1994 book, *Autobiography of a Face,* explores the alienation she felt as a result of her appearance, the strategies she used to cope with her visible differences, and the complicated feelings she harbored about herself. Students should note that Grealy's personal narrative is both objective and analytical; she does not succumb to self-pity in her writing. Instead, she analyzes how her deformity—and other people's responses to it—affected her identity.

Encourage your students to examine the significance of the masks—both real and metaphorical—in this piece. Masks are a common element of almost every culture. Because they obscure the face, they allow the wearer to hide his or her identity or temporarily assume the identity of someone (or something) else. Especially in the context of masquerade or carnival, when disguise is customary, the anonymity masks provide generally fosters a sense of freedom and emboldens wearers to behave in ways that social conventions normally prohibit or at least discourage. At the same time, masks afford wearers an opportunity to alter outward appearances to better reflect who they believe themselves to be.

In this narrative, they serve to temporarily conceal Grealy's deformity, but they also demonstrate a contrast between her reality and that of the people who surround her. For Grealy, a mask—whether it's a scarf that hides her jaw, a hat that covers her baldness, a plastic image that gives her a fictional identity, or a turtleneck that makes her scars less visible—symbolizes temporary normalcy. Other children view her disfigurement as the real mask—a monster mask—something that separates her from them and renders her less than human (par. 2). By disguising her deformity, Grealy discovers that she is suddenly free to interact with people without judgment on their parts or self-consciousness on her own. Her identity is so wrapped up in her feelings of ugliness that hiding her appearance lets her imagine herself differently, if only for a short while.

Interrogating Assumptions

Grealy's cancer diagnosis, multiple surgeries, and endless rounds of chemotherapy as depicted in this piece aren't characterized by the same rawness and suffering that she has to endure in the outside world. Periodic hospitalizations are treated as a haven from the torture she has to face at school, and in this piece, the pain of the illness is eclipsed by that imposed on her by her own peers. Grealy's deformity is her reality, but it isn't her identity until it is made so by others. She is in a stage of development in which physical attractiveness and sexual desirability are paramount, comprising the very definition of self-worth and the standard for deserving happiness. As somebody who does not meet that societal criteria, her lack of desirability is reinforced and infused into her identity by others.

Writing about Cultural Practices

This assignment calls for a close reading and critical analysis of a single essay. Although students should feel free to consult outside sources, to include personal reflection, and to develop their own arguments, their responses should be grounded in Grealy's own evaluation of her experience. Refer them back to the chapter introduction's discussion of the three major assumptions surrounding identity formation, and encourage them to incorporate those ideas and questions into their analyses.

Additional Resources

Nonfiction

Lucy Grealy, *As Seen on TV* (2000)   Among the essays in this collection is "Mirrorings," an early formulation of the issues Grealy confronts in *Autobiography of a Face.*

Ann Patchett, *Truth and Beauty* (2004)   Patchett's memoir follows her friendship with Lucy Grealy, from their meeting in college through the successes and depressions of Grealy's later years.

Poem

Paul Laurence Dunbar, "We Wear the Mask" (1896)   Dunbar uses the metaphor of the mask to describe the double existence forced on African Americans.

Film

Mask (1985)   A boy with a severe facial deformity and an unconventional family (Cher plays his biker mother) struggles to lead a normal life.

Web

Truth and Beauty: A Tale of Friendship, http://www.npr.org/templates/story/story.php?storyId=1892114   Visitors can listen to sound files of Ann Patchett's appearance on the NPR show *All Things Considered,* as well as an interview with and memorials to Lucy Grealy.

September 11 Tattoos (p. 49)

For the past 150 years or so, Americans have traditionally mourned their dead by visiting cemeteries. Toward the end of the twentieth century, alternative expressions of grief emerged. These alternatives include urban murals, roadside memorials, T-shirts (see Jenn Shreve, "A Fitting Memorial: The Commemorative T-Shirt," p. 243), and commemorative websites. For most of the close to 3,000 victims of the September 11 attacks, there are no graves, and so Americans have had to find other ways to express their grief. The tattoos pictured in this chapter represent another alternative expression of mourning. They not only memorialize the individual people killed on September 11 but also mourn the loss of a culture that was forced to redefine itself in the wake of the tragedy.

The patriotic imagery of these tattoos—especially the undulating American flag—illustrates how personally many Americans responded to the terror attacks on their country. Patriotism, of course, is a way of identifying with a large group and connecting to a culture. In these images, that cultural identity is closely tied to more personal expressions. Two of the images invoke the Christian concept of God (note the hands of God in the second image and the biblical quote in the third). These images may be interpreted as personal symbols of comfort, as visual arguments in response to an attack that was waged largely on religious grounds, or as both. The same two images incorporate ideas of family into the concept of patriotism and mourning ("brotherhood" and "brothers and sisters"). Each of these tattoos is located on the wearer's bicep—a cultural symbol of strength. Encourage your students to take a close look at the symbolism of the first tattoo in particular. The shadow of the airplane adapts the Victorian use of silhouettes to portray departed loved ones. Even more interesting is the yellow rose: A symbol of both friendship and lost love in American culture, in Islamic culture it's an image of deceit and treachery.

Many Americans had a visceral response to the events of September 11, 2001. It may be productive to have your students examine the tattoos in the context of body art. How are they a physical manifestation of emotional pain? Do the images express solidarity, defiance, grief, anger, or something else? Are they an attempt to assert identity or to negotiate it—or maybe a little bit of both? To what extent, if any, might the wearers be using their tattoos to retain their pre–September 11 identities?

Writing about Cultural Practices

Visually oriented students will be tempted to focus most of their energies for this assignment on creating artistic masterpieces with their photo essays. Although you should encourage students to experiment with layout and design, remind them that this is a written assignment. Its purpose is to get students to read images critically in the context of cultural identity formation (point them back, if necessary, to the assumptions outlined in the chapter introduction). Cultural analysis will be easier for your students if they choose images that show the tattoos in a larger context—gender, clothing, physical surroundings, and the like. Where to obtain the images might pose a challenge for some students. You may want to suggest that they cut and paste photographs from a newspaper or magazine (fashion, sports, and music magazines are particularly rich sources). Students with Internet access might search image galleries on the Web for photographs of a particular tattoo theme that interests them.

Keep in mind that some students have better design skills (and better technology resources) than others do. Assure your class that the content of their photo essays is more important than the aesthetic appeal.

Additional Resources

Nonfiction

Martha Cooper and Joseph Sciorra, *R.I.P.: Memorial Wall Art* (1994)   The photographs in this book capture murals painted throughout New York City in memory of lost loved ones, often the victims of urban violence.

Holly Everett, *Roadside Crosses in Contemporary Culture* (2002)   Everett's study of roadside memorials explores the functions they serve for grieving families and for the culture as a whole.

Fiction

Jonathan Safran Foer, *Extremely Loud and Incredibly Close* (2005)   After losing his father on September 11, the precocious young hero goes on a quest. He searches New York to find the lock that fits a key found among his father's possessions.

Web

Needled, http://www.needled.com/   An online magazine of tattoo culture, *Needled* explores the history and trends of tattooing.

September 11, 2001, Victims, http://www.september11victims.com/ september11victims/   This site contains names and profiles of victims of the September 11 attacks.

Gloria Anzaldúa, **How to Tame a Wild Tongue** (p. 53)

Gloria Anzaldúa wrote *Borderlands/La Frontera,* in which this essay was originally published, at the height of the multiculturalism debates that preoccupied American academia and cultural politics in the 1980s. As many teachers and columnists pushed to expand the canon to include works by non-Anglo writers and to celebrate the diverse cultures that comprise American life, others argued that multiculturalism threatened to fracture American society. Anzaldúa's response to this argument is that attempting to acculturate minority groups fractures individual identities and weakens American culture as a whole.

At several points in her essay, Anzaldúa raises the question of what makes a person—or a culture—"American." Firoozeh Dumas, in the paired essay "The 'F Word'" (p. 60), raises the same issue. You may want to begin classroom discussion by asking students to tackle this question directly. Divide them into small groups, and instruct them to brainstorm a list of qualities they think of as distinctly "American." Compile a list of their ideas on the blackboard, and discuss the results. Why is it so difficult to define what "American" is? Who gets to decide, and why? What happens to a person who isn't "American" enough?

For Anzaldúa, the answers to this question are as political as they are intensely personal. Her struggles with the dominant culture's attempts at "taming" her "tongue" are infused with an acute awareness of racial, class, and gender issues. Whole cultures, she argues, are being destroyed by pressures to assimilate, and individual identities are being compromised in the process. She considers it far better to embrace the mixed languages and identities that are formed when different cultures come in contact with each other. Language and identity are, in Anzaldúa's formation, inseparable; to deny a person the freedom to use her language is to deny who she is. At the same time, Anzaldúa points out that minority cultures often manipulate languages to create and affirm the value of group identity (see pars. 12–13, 17). Individuals negotiate multiple facets of their identities through the way they communicate with each other. Her use of untranslated Spanish throughout the essay underscores this political use of language, as well as the feelings of alienation and frustration that come with not identifying with a dominant form of expression. If students resent the writer's refusal to speak their language, remind them that's exactly her point.

Interrogating Assumptions

Most of us navigate among several cultures. Anzaldúa's essay illustrates that every one of those cultures impacts our identity, and they often compete with each other. She points out that our identities are influenced by culture whether we like it or not, and that cultural influences on identity can be harmful both for individuals and society at large. Members of maligned minority groups, for example, often internalize and perpetuate the dominant culture's negative valuations of their culture (see pars. 22–25). Anzaldúa stresses that the mixed cultures that form in contact zones are beneficial and desirable; she is adamantly opposed to forced assimilation in either direction. "Taming a wild tongue" is a metaphor for born attributes and acculturation (if necessary, remind your students that a tongue is both a body part and a language); Anzaldúa's argument is that forcing acculturation is a form of cultural and personal violence.

Writing about Cultural Practices

Monolingual students may resist this assignment, insisting that they speak only one language; others might be intimidated by Anzaldúa's fluency in eight linguistic variations of English and Spanish. You may need to explain to them that even if they speak only English, they adapt their vocabulary, tone, and level of formality to the different situations they find themselves in on a daily basis. "Versions" of a language might include slang, workplace jargon, IM or other forms of high-tech dialect, rapidity of speech, even volume.

As they write their analyses, students should use Anzaldúa's essay as a model for their approach without feeling they have to approximate the depth and complexity of cultural analysis that she is so well known for. Although the assignment asks for an ostensibly personal essay, tell your students that you expect them to analyze their experiences in the context of cultural influences on identity formation. Like Anzaldúa, students should incorporate specific examples and explore what their language choices reveal about who they are.

Additional Resources

Nonfiction

Casey Miller and Kate Swift, *The Handbook of Nonsexist Writing* (1980) Miller and Swift analyze instances of gendered language in English and suggest ways of writing without bias.

Richard Rodriguez, *Hunger of Memory* (1982) Rodriguez's memoir describes his bilingual childhood in California.

AnaLouise Keating, *EntreMundos/AmongWorlds: New Perspectives on Gloria Anzaldúa* (2005) A multidisciplinary collection of writings on Anzaldúa's work, this book addresses both her visionary theories and her work for social justice.

Film

Spanglish (2004) A woman emigrates from Mexico with her daughter and finds work with a Los Angeles family. Overcoming the language barrier is only one of the difficulties she encounters in their dysfunctional home.

Web

Multilingualism in Cyberspace, http://www.unesco.org/webworld/multilingualism UNESCO's site contains statistics and documents on the rise of Internet multilingualism.

Firoozeh Dumas, **The "F Word"** (p. 60)

Firoozeh Dumas's humorous reflections on her immigrant experience reveal an important aspect of the born attributes of identity. As she explains, the identity she was born with takes on different implications depending on cultural context. Her ethnicity has a wholly different meaning in the United States than it would have had in her native country: Names that were a source of strength and pride in Iran became, in America, a catalyst for teasing and embarrassment. Cultural influences force Dumas to redefine herself to fit into new environments, such as grade school, college, the job market, and motherhood. Her choices, however, don't always have the wished-for consequences, so she continuously redefines herself according to her environment, her life situation, and her desires.

Dumas's experience illustrates that something as simple as a name can be fraught with implications for identity. As was the case for Gloria Anzaldúa, Dumas's born identity markers are belittled by the dominant American culture.

Whereas Anzaldúa fiercely resists assimilation, however, Dumas attempts to embrace it, with mixed results. Despite their different approaches, both writers find themselves in the position of negotiating multiple identities that are tied to language. And both discover that linguistic choices can pose social, economic, and political barriers for members of minority cultures.

Dumas responds to Americans' difficulties with her name by pointing out the flaws of American language as well as the ways in which resistance to diversity weakens American culture as a whole. Although her tone is humorous, encourage your students to analyze the purpose and effect of her lighthearted approach. Is her point really all that different from Anzaldúa's?

Writing about Cultural Practices

This assignment asks for a short essay that explores the meaning of something usually taken for granted. Despite food's centrality to everyday life, most Americans don't give much thought to what culinary habits imply about a culture. Because of this, the hardest task for students might be identifying an "American" food. Don't let them get caught up in the issue of food origins: Pizza could well be considered typically American despite its Italian background, and for some, tacos are as American as apple pie. In fact, choosing food items with foreign backgrounds might lead students to discover that objects and practices, as well as people, can be acculturated.

A successful student essay will contain three elements. First, it will identify a "typically American" food and describe it (and the ways in which it is produced and consumed) in enough detail that somebody unfamiliar with it can understand what it is. Second, it will explain the student's reasons for classifying the food as American. Finally, it will make some attempt at interpreting the food as a cultural artifact. Students should feel free to try to emulate Dumas's lighthearted and humorous tone, but a more serious approach would also work well.

Additional Resources

Nonfiction

Marjane Satrapi, *Embroideries* (2005)   A follow-up to Satrapi's acclaimed *Persepolis* and *Persepolis 2, Embroideries* focuses on the author's female relatives and the stories of their sexual lives.

Azedeh Moaveni, *Lipstick Jihad: A Memoir of Growing Up Iranian in America and American in Iran* (2005)   Moving between cultures, the author describes the tensions between her American upbringing and her fascination with her family's life in Iran.

Samuel P. Huntington, *Who Are We?* (2004)   In this controversial polemic, Huntington argues in favor of assimilation and of maintaining a unifying American identity.

Film

House of Sand and Fog (2003)   A former Iranian army officer and his wife enter a legal battle with a young American woman over the rights to a house. Shohreh Aghdashloo, whose dialogue in the movie mixes Farsi with English, was nominated for an Academy Award for her performance.

Television

My American Girls: A Dominican Story (2001)   Part of the *P.O.V.* series, this documentary aired on PBS and is now available on video. Filmmaker Aaron Matthews follows the story of the Ortiz family, first-generation immigrants who dream of returning to their homeland and their three American-born daughters.

Russell Thornton, **What the Census Doesn't Count** (p. 65)

Thornton's assertion that race "is a social notion, not a biological reality" may not be as obvious to students as it is to the writer. You may, therefore, want to begin discussion of this essay by explaining the idea of race as a social construction. Students may not know, for example, that Irish, Italian, and Jewish heritage excluded people from categorization as "white" until fairly recently, that "a single drop" of black ancestry legally classified a person as black through the first half of the twentieth century, or that several cultures outside of the United States have far more complex systems of racial categorization than Americans' rigid black/white/native/Asian/Latino rubric.

This essay makes a strong case against the assumption that identity is a matter of choice. Although the 2000 census let mixed-race Americans choose which race (one or several) they most identified with, Thornton argues that self-identification is largely meaningless. As he sees it, how others categorize a person has more social and political consequences than how that person categorizes him- or herself. The issue is important because census results influence public policy, political representation, and public funding.

To help students understand Thornton's point about social constructions of individual identities, encourage them to apply his analysis to the personal experiences described by the other writers in this chapter. Kathy Wilson, for example, sees herself as thoroughly feminine, but her appearance leads others to define her quite differently; Gloria Anzaldúa struggles to assert her multifaceted cultural identity in the face of Anglo assumptions of a monolithic Latino culture; Firoozeh Dumas successfully convinces others of her Americanness only to find herself feeling like a fraud. Whose definition of identity prevails in each of these cases? And how does that affect the person being defined?

Writing about Cultural Practices

This fairly involved assignment requires that your students do some well-planned field research and conduct a sophisticated analysis of their results. It will be most successful if you construct it as an extended group project. Unless they're experienced pollsters, students will need your help preparing an effective questionnaire, so consider drafting it as an in-class project, brainstorming the questions and working together to organize them into something manageable for respondents and easily distilled into measurable statistics for a table or graph. Make each student responsible for distributing the questionnaire to a specific number of friends, and require everyone in the class to fill out a questionnaire themselves (keep the responses anonymous). Once the results are in, divide responsibility for compiling the results among small groups or individual students, and then distribute the completed data to everyone in the class. You may have your students write analyses of the results as individual papers or assign small groups to present their interpretations as oral reports.

Additional Resources

Television

Family Guy, "Peter Griffin: Husband, Father, Brother . . . ?" (2001)   In season 3, episode 42, Irish-Catholic Peter Griffin discovers that he has a black ancestor and attempts to join the neighborhood's African American civic club. Meanwhile, his son embraces black popular culture.

America Beyond the Color Line (2005)   In this PBS series, Henry Louis Gates visits African American communities throughout the United States and interviews some of the most influential figures in the country about the state of black America.

Nonfiction

Nelson George, *Hip Hop America* (1999)   Hip hop is a cultural force that crosses race and class lines. George surveys the history of the music and addresses its powerful influence on American youth.

Joseph Lelyveld, *How Race Is Lived in America* (2001)   This series of essays, first published in the *New York Times,* addresses some of the complicated issues surrounding race in twenty-first-century America.

Web

Fair Vote, http://www.fairvote.org/index.php?page=567   Fair Vote's page on racial and ethnic minorities provides reports and articles on the representation of minority groups in elections.

Michelle Lee, **The Fashion Victim's Ten Commandments** (p. 69)

The flip, sarcastic tone that Lee uses to make her points about fashion may lead many of your students to dismiss this excerpt from *Fashion Victim* as something as frivolous as the high-fashion world that Lee mocks. You'll need to press them to tease out the serious implications of the examples Lee provides. Her cultural critique is subversively implicit, and it will take some work to help students see that she is making some important points about how fashion marketing affects American identities. It will be worthwhile, also, to remind your students of the context in which Lee usually writes: Fashion magazines, especially those directed at women, have been harshly criticized for deliberately fostering negative self-images among their readers. Students should consider whether Lee, who frequently publishes in these magazines, is attempting to address that issue with her book.

Some historical context may help your students take this piece more seriously. Many of the dynamics Lee decries have been in evidence since the advent of mass-market fashions in the 1910s. From the earliest days of machine-made fashions, working class women have spent beyond their means to acquire clothing that signaled their middle-class aspirations (and many found that looking the part did indeed help them to raise their social standing). Children of immigrants sometimes embraced frivolous clothing to prove their assimilation to American culture, to distance themselves from their parents' old-world values, and to influence how others saw them. Again, buying into fashion mores could help them to navigate often-hostile terrain. Haute couture designers of the early twentieth century borrowed ideas from working class clothing practices in much the same way Lee describes for the late twentieth century. And as early as the 1850s, famous designers loaned clothes to socialites as a marketing strategy for popularizing their latest styles.

As one of the most visible identity markers that people can choose for themselves, clothing is particularly important in forming one's sense of self. Because it constantly evolves, fashion also underscores the fluidity of identity. But as Lee points out, larger cultural forces play a role in the clothing choices we make, and other people's interpretations of clothing's meaning ultimately have more force than the wearer's intentions.

Writing about Cultural Practices

Both of the assignments that follow "The Fashion Victim's Ten Commandments" elicit imaginative writing in a playful format.

If you want to encourage your students to experiment with their writing and to take creative risks, structure the first assignment (question 5) as an in-class writing exercise rather than as a formal paper. For an extra dose of playfulness, you might randomly assign students to describe classmates' shoes and make a game of identifying their wearers based on the written descriptions.

The second assignment (question 6) would work especially well as a group writing project. Rather than putting students in the often-awkward position of having to critically analyze their own work as it compares to a professional sample, remove some of the pressure by letting the students distance themselves from the lists being compared. Have your class draft a list of antifashion commandments as a group; then send them home to write individual papers comparing them to Lee's commandments.

Additional Resources

Nonfiction

Teri Agins, *The End of Fashion: How Marketing Changed the Clothing Business Forever* (2000)   Agins's history of the fashion industry analyzes why a world once ruled by couture designers is now taking its cues from mass-market goods.

Television

What Not to Wear   Hosts Clinton and Stacy surprise ill-dressed subjects with secret tapes of their fashion mistakes before helping them to shop for new wardrobes.

Film

Unzipped (1995)   This documentary about Isaac Mizrahi follows the designer through a year in the fashion world, culminating with a runway show of "'50s cheesecake meets Eskimo fake fur."

Magazine

Lucky   The first magazine explicitly about shopping, *Lucky* focuses on women's clothes and accessories. It was followed by *Cargo* for menswear and *Domino* for home decor.

Shannon Wheeler, **I Hated Journey** (p. 77)

Despite its extraordinary popularity in the early 1980s, Journey no longer gets much airplay on commercial radio, not even on stations with a classic rock format. If students report that they don't know who Journey is, you may need to play part of one of its more overwrought songs ("Don't Stop Believing" and "Open Arms" come to mind) so students will understand why someone might react to its music as Wheeler's characters do.

The target of the characters' dislike, however, is not as important as how their dislike helps to shape their identities. As Wheeler's cartoon demonstrates, we often define ourselves by what we're not. Friends (and entire cultures) tend to bond over shared enemies. Ask your students to consider both the positive and the negative influences of this form of social bonding. On the one hand, it can give people who don't fit into the larger culture a sense of belonging and camaraderie. But defining oneself in opposition to others also creates negative social tensions and self-imposed alienation.

In addition to revealing the impact of personal tastes on sense of self and interpersonal relationships, Wheeler's cartoon reveals the fluid nature of identity. Despite his determined dislike of Journey as a teenager, years later the character is confused and distressed to find that he now likes the band because its music fosters a happy nostalgia. His ambivalence also underscores the subversive ways in which cultural forces influence personal taste and identity. Even when we resist it, popular culture defines us, often in ways that we can't anticipate.

Writing about Cultural Practices

This assignment calls for a personal essay with some critical distance to its subject matter. If you'd rather not read a pile of essays about "why Britney Spears sucks," tell your students that their responses should be not praise nor criticism of a fad itself, but rather an exploration of their personal experiences with it. Encourage them, as well, to be flexible in choosing a fad to write about. They may feel strongly, for example, about something that is popular among their peers right now; they may also have experienced a localized trend that didn't apply to popular culture outside of their immediate neighborhood or circle of friends. Finally, remind them that they can write about either rejecting a trend or participating in it; assure them that you won't judge them for their choices.

For a model essay about the impact of personal tastes and nonconformity, refer students to Kathy Wilson's "Dude Looks Like a Lady" (p. 21). Remind them, too, that they don't need to comment on the cartoon or any of the readings in the chapter as they craft their essays. The point of the exercise is to get them thinking about their own experiences, not to prepare a critical analysis of other written works.

Additional Resources

Nonfiction

David Camp and Steven Daly, *The Rock Snob's Dictionary: An Essential Lexicon of Rockological Knowledge* (2005)   An A-to-Z compendium of rock-and-roll minutiae for music fanatics.

Film

Ghost World (2004)   Thora Birch and Scarlet Johansson play recent high school graduates who make a lifestyle out of scorning the habits and interests of their peers.

Web

Too Much Coffee Man, http://www.tmcm.com/   Shannon Wheeler's comics on politics and culture are collected on this website.

Vote for the Worst, http://www.votefortheworst.com   Visitors to this site can cast a vote for the worst contestants on popular reality shows.

Fametracker Fame Audit, http://www.fametracker.com/fame_audit/   Website authors cover the assets and liabilities of popular celebrities, frequently ruling that their fame is out of proportion to their talent.

Mixing Words and Images:
Creating an Identi-kit (p. 81)

As one culminating project for chapter 1, this assignment asks students to explore for themselves many of the central questions raised by the readings and the chapter introduction. What makes us who we are? To what extent is identity culturally determined? To what extent is identity a matter of personal choice? Whatever else has come across in the reading, discussion, and writing students will have done up until this assignment, one point they will have encountered is that the concept of identity is no longer understood as fixed or stable over a person's lifetime. As a postmodern concept that is central to cultural studies, the chapter speaks of identity as being multiple, flexible, and fluid. It is precisely this understanding that makes the identi-kit assignment such a pleasurable project for students. It gives them an opportunity to investigate the extent to which their own sense of identity is a playful negotiation between social norms and personal choices.

When introducing this project, you may want to use class time to help students generate ideas for their identi-kits. For instance, you may use the following questions in an in-class brainstorming activity: What are 10 adjectives your closest friends would use to describe you? What are six items that you almost never leave the house without? What are five activities you love? List at least 15 different identity labels that currently apply to you. Answers to this last question might include: brother, parent, student, captain of my baseball team, skateboarder, girlfriend, *South Park* fan, and so on. To encourage students to generate as many ideas as possible, let them know you won't collect their written responses to these questions.

As students begin constructing their identi-kits, consider establishing a few ground rules. First, while students can design their identi-kits in a variety of ways, the pictures must all share one visual requirement: An image or representation of their face and body must be present, if not central. Without this requirement, some students may too easily take an "everything but the kitchen sink" approach to the assignment, creating collages that are unfocused and lacking a central theme. Second, you will need to remind students that these collages are meant to focus on *one* aspect of their identity, not to be a complete self-portrait. Lastly, the identi-kit pictures can be as high- or low-tech as you wish. Some students may want to use computer programs to design their pictures; others may hand-draw most of the elements of their pictures. Most students will use a collage method, cutting and pasting together images from magazines, photos, and online sources. If they are using personal photos, tell students to make photocopies of favorite pictures and cut those up to create their collages. No one should have to destroy precious memories for this project.

As you plan the number of class days that will be necessary to complete this assignment, be sure to account for the double-drafting process. First, students need to draft their identi-kits; then they will need time to draft the descriptive analysis essay. Both elements of this assignment should be given adequate space in your schedule.

Connecting to Culture: Suggestions for Writing (p. 82)

The writing assignments that conclude the chapter offer students an opportunity to synthesize the ideas they've encountered in the readings and to make some conclusions about the assumptions outlined in the chapter introduction.

How to Belong: A Critical Analysis of Cool

This project asks students to write an academic essay modeled on a professional writer's cultural analysis. Their responses should be founded on detailed observation and a careful critique of what they find. Although students may refer to White or to other essayists in the chapter, it is more important that they form an opinion based on their own observations and defend their positions coherently.

Looking the Part: Deconstructing Personal Fashion

This assignment uses visual analysis to examine cultural artifacts, personal choices, and social consequences. Students will need to assume the role of self-critic; if that makes some uncomfortable, offer them the option of describing and analyzing a friend's or family member's "look," reminding them to be charitable in their judgments. Responses should combine descriptive narrative and critical analysis and center on an arguable thesis.

Interrogating Assumptions: What Makes Us Who We Are?

The most formal of the writing projects in this chapter, this final assignment calls for a text-based comparative analysis that synthesizes ideas from the chapter and several individual readings. To ensure coherence, encourage students to select readings that are closely related thematically as well as in the manner that they address assumptions about identity. If you've assigned any of the Interrogating Assumptions questions that follow the readings in the chapter, allow your students to use their responses as starting points for their drafts. A successful student essay will posit a thesis about one of the assumptions and use the readings to support it, rather than simply compare and contrast several selections.

2 Community

... or, are these your people?

The tension between individualism and communality has long perplexed American society. It was the central dilemma faced by the transcendental movement of the nineteenth century, and it has affected public policy debates on everything from tax law to gay marriage. The issue is one of balance: What do communities provide for their members, and what do individual members owe their communities? Although there are no easy answers, Americans have always attempted to structure communities of their own design. From colonial charters to utopian experiments to online chat rooms, the effort to carve out interpersonal niches is an enduring hallmark of American culture.

Because questions of community and identity are closely intertwined you'll find it effective to teach this chapter in conjunction with the chapter on identity. Several of the readings in chapter 1 (especially those by White, Grealy, Anzaldúa, Thornton, and Lee) touch on the themes explored in this chapter, and several of the readings in this chapter (including those by Rodriguez, Angelou, and Leonard) will complicate students' understanding of identity formation. The assignments in the two chapters complement each other nicely; in many cases, you might encourage students to use responses to questions in chapter 1 as starting points for their writing about community.

With a little encouragement, your students should be able to identify several communities to which they currently belong. They might name their families, their ethnic or racial affiliations, their hometowns and current neighborhoods, fellow college students, their majors, work colleagues, sexual orientations, listservs and message forums, political affiliations, fan bases, and clubs, to list just a few examples. Although community affiliations may be assigned or chosen, they affect a person's sense of self and color most aspects of daily life, whether or not that influence is recognized. Before you ask students to read the chapter introduction, you may want them to explore, as a class or individually as a preliminary journal assignment, what assumptions they currently hold about their own communities. Brainstorm as a group what "community" means, what it provides for its members, and what it expects of its members in turn.

Because the central assumptions outlined in the chapter's introduction form the basis for analyzing its readings, spend some time discussing them in class. Use the questions that follow each discussion of an assumption to explore the concept with your students. You might want to ask whether your students agree or disagree with the outlined assumptions, as well as what other assumptions about community they can identify. Discuss with your class, also, how these assumptions function in American culture: Who holds them? What purposes do they serve? Are they helpful or harmful? And how do students see them played out in their personal lives and in the world around them?

As they work through the chapter, students will examine different conceptions of how communities function and piece together their own definitions of what community is. The Examining the Everyday activity that opens the chapter encourages them to take an initial step in that direction, basing their definitions solely on their experiences with a small group of activity partners. Keep in mind that there are no incorrect answers to the questions posed in the text. The point of the initial project is to get students thinking analytically and to question their own assumptions. For an interesting twist, consider asking students to revisit their responses, perhaps to rewrite them, after they have read and responded to several of the readings in the chapter.

All of the readings in this chapter explore one or several of the three main assumptions outlined in the introduction—communities provide stability, communities serve individual needs, communities are accepting. Kathleen Norris takes advantage of her outsider status to develop her argument about small-town life. Richard Rodriguez and Maya Angelou combine personal narrative and cultural criticism to explore racial communities. Mim Udovitch's disturbing journalistic look at the online "pro-ana" community demonstrates the potentially destructive influences of some communities. Andrew Leonard and Jennifer Bishop Fulwiler dispute the authenticity of online communities, raising important questions about the definition of "community" in the process. Cultural anthropologist John A. Hostetler and intellectual-historian David Brooks offer scholarly studies of the function and implications of some communities, a recent example of which is portrayed in Peter Granser and Bill Donahue's photo essay, "The Land of the Setting Sun."

Additional Resources

Nonfiction

Robert D. Putnam, *Bowling Alone: The Collapse and Revival of American Communities* (2001)   Putnam received national attention after the publication of *Bowling Alone*, in which he argues that Americans are losing their connection with the people around them.

Fiction

Jeffrey Eugenides, *The Virgin Suicides* (1993)   The suicides of the five Lisbon sisters take on a mythic significance for their classmates, who search for signs of meaning in the tragedy.

Film

It's a Wonderful Life (1947)   In this Frank Capra classic, Jimmy Stewart plays a man who, believing he is worth more dead than alive, attempts to commit suicide on Christmas Eve. An angel intervenes and shows Stewart a vision of how the world would be without him in it.

Pleasantville (1998)   Two siblings are transported to the idyllic world of a television show. While one plays by the small-town rules, the other disrupts the workings of the place by doing things her own way.

Television

Town Haul   Former *Trading Spaces* designer Genevieve Gorder attempts to make over a whole town, rallying residents to help choose, plan, and execute major renovations.

Gilmore Girls   Set in the quirky small town of Stars Hollow, this comedy centers on the unconventional relationship of a thirtysomething mother and her teenage daughter.

Rosario Morales and Aurora Levins Morales, Ending Poem (p. 95)

Written by two Puerto Rican American, Jewish women, "Ending Poem" takes one family's history and breaks it into several parts. Although a mother and daughter penned this poem together, your students will likely find that their voices aren't immediately distinguishable. It may become apparent as they read on that the poem's perspective isn't only from that of its writers but from a weave of generations. Taking this approach, pieces of a long history of daily life and tradition are rearranged and intentionally out of order, but by the end of the poem, they create a cohesive picture for one small community.

Students should examine this piece, keeping in mind that the ideas they have—even the things they take for granted—about their own heritage are probably not unlike the approach of the poem. The broader cultural assumptions that are held about their communities on the outside may not be as prominent in their minds as the fragments of personal history that they carry with them every day.

The crux of the piece is not necessarily that of direct experience, though, but rather how a mishmash of voices and histories creates a community, something "whole." In this way, Morales and Levins Morales's work challenges the assumption that communities provide stability; in fact, they can sometimes do anything but. The family community is one built on a long history of changes and the sidestepping of cultural stereotypes, and it is these contradictions that complicate stability and routine. In short, challenging assumptions—knowingly or unknowingly—about culture and tradition is the family's common ground. It's the life of the poem and of the family.

Writing about Cultural Practices

Both of the assignments that follow "Ending Poem" ask students to examine history, and how the past has influenced who—and where—they are today. The first assignment encourages students to take a creative approach to looking back at their families and at their own lives. The second asks them to research and report on their school's history and traditions, examining the impact these things have made on what the institution is today. Each assignment centers on the idea of heritage, prompting students to think critically about what stands out as significant in their lives and communities, and why.

Successful student work for both assignments will, in addition to relating and articulating important events, examine their outcome. What about their family history makes them who they are today? How is it different for their relatives? Is it different at all? Also, what kind of emphasis does their school place on its tradition? Did tradition attract them to the school, or is it even important? As they answer these questions, encourage your students to consider them in the context of community. Where do they draw the line between their individuality and their community? In other words, is there a time or place where one ceases to influence the other?

Additional Resources

Nonfiction

Marjorie Agosin, ed., *House of Memory: Stories of Jewish Women Writers of Latin America* (1999)   In 22 selections, the authors relate their memories of the places they've left behind.

Film

Jai (2005)   The Boston Jewish Film Festival describes *Jai* as a "touching and emotional short film that depicts the reaction of two Mexican children to the sight of numbers tattooed by the Nazis on the arms of their elderly immigrant grandparents."

John A. Hostetler, **The Amish Charter** (p. 99)

Shunning society at large because it does not share the group's priorities and threatens to undermine its values, the Amish have established and maintained one of the few alternatives to modern American life. The community's survival depends on isolation and every member's strict adherence to its principles. As Hostetler suggests, their long-term survival stems from their commitment to traditions and their willingness to remove any members who fail to uphold the community's standards.

The Amish are interested not in growing their ranks but in preserving a rigid system designed to serve the needs of established members. Membership in this community is a conscious decision taken very seriously by everybody involved. Although the Amish are born into their community, individuals cannot become full members until they reach adulthood and formally agree to adhere to their church's rules and principles. Amish rules and taboos are built on a paradoxical relationship between the individual and the community: Individuals must subordinate their needs and desires to those of the community, but in the end the community's purpose is to serve its individual members by assuring their acceptance into the Kingdom of God. Only through self-denial and strict obedience to community standards can the individual hope to achieve salvation, which the Amish view as the purpose of life on earth.

Amish rules and mores, which to students may seem petty at first glance, promote the community's goal of individual salvation. Amish strictures emphasize to every member that worldly living is temporary and is not to be embraced as an end in itself. Similarly, long-standing customs and traditions establish the community's separation from the outside world and symbolize the otherworldly focus of Amish life. In rejecting all things decorative and luxurious, the *Ordnung* keeps members' focus on their faith and on their purpose in this world—to prepare for the next.

Interrogating Assumptions

From the Amish perspective, failure to follow tradition threatens not only individual salvation but also the very survival of the community. Requiring strict adherence to simple rules gives the community some level of control over individual members' behavior; in doing so, it also makes community principles and beliefs a matter of personal habit. Community stability is the whole purpose of the *Ordnung*, but note as well that the rules cannot be established without unanimous consensus and that they are subject to change. Stability is so central to Amish society that they will remove any members who threaten it. Banishment may strike your students as harsh, but it is intended to help the individual, not only by encouraging repentance but also by protecting the community's founding principles from dilution. By excommunicating dissenters, the Amish can ensure the stability of their community and protect the faithful from harmful influences.

Writing about Cultural Practices

Both of the assignments that follow Hostetler's essay encourage students to assume the role of cultural anthropologist. In each case, they will need to analyze the social purpose of restrictions on individuals' behaviors. The first assignment asks students to assess an existing set of written rules to which they are expected to adhere; the second one encourages students to articulate unwritten rules (they may want to refer to "The Fashion Victim's Ten Commandments," on p. 69, as a model).

For both assignments, students will need to write a thorough description or overview of a code of conduct (whether existing or invented) before they embark on their analyses of the rules themselves. They will also need to make an attempt to explain the larger social functions of community rules, considering, for example, (1) why individuals are willing to ascribe to codes of behavior that restrict their freedoms and (2) what benefits community membership confers on its individual members.

Additional Resources

Nonfiction

Eric Brende, *Better Off: Flipping the Switch on Technology* (2004)   A former MIT graduate student writes about the year he took off to live and work with a group of people he calls the "Minimites."

Bill McKibben, *Enough* (2003)   In McKibben's cautionary book on the dangers of genetic engineering, he takes the Amish as an example of a community that, rather than rejecting technology on principle, has consciously evaluated new technologies for how they will have an impact on daily life.

Film

Witness (1985)   Harrison Ford plays a detective who goes undercover in an Amish community to solve a murder.

Television

Amish in the City   In an unusual twist on *The Real World,* Amish teens on "rumspringa" live in a Los Angeles house with a group of city kids.

Web

Amish Country News, http://www.amishnews.com/index.htm   This Pennsylvania tourism newsletter is purportedly vetted by members of the Amish community.

Mim Udovitch, **A Secret Society of the Starving** (p. 109)

Considering the high rate of eating disorders among teenage girls and young women, the themes of this reading may cause severe discomfort for some of your students who may have personal experience with anorexia and bulimia (their own, or that of a friend or family member). To keep the discussion productive, try to steer it away from graphic representations of eating disorders, personal examples, or negative judgments. Instead, do what you can to focus your students on the social aspects of the pro-ana world and the ways in which it illustrates the dynamics of community in general.

This article makes clear that communities can be destructive influences on their individual members. Your students' natural impulse will be to start identifying other examples of harmful communities. While you should allow them to extend Udovitch's observations to multiple harmful cases, don't let them get mired in negative examples. Remind them that people generally seek out support communities for positive reasons. Support groups provide something that their members desperately need but can't get elsewhere. Work with your students to puzzle out what that something is. Press them to uncover the dynamics that draw people to these communities in the first place and to consider what the pro-ana online community reveals about the personal and social functions of communities. What benefits do members gain from joining groups that at some level they know to be harmful to them?

Writing about Cultural Practices

This assignment asks students to apply the chapter's three assumptions to an isolated community of manageable size. Students should start by identifying the community they want to explore. Although they may be interested in writing about a group to which they belong, point out to them that they will have an easier time being truthful and objective if they choose a community that they are not a part of. Encourage your class to follow Udovitch's lead and interview several members of the group they choose to examine. They might ask their informants why they joined a group, what they gain from it, and how they participate in it; they should also ask for examples of specific instances of peer pressure and how their interviewees responded to it.

Once the data is gathered, writers will need to select the example of peer pressure that best illustrates what they've learned about a group. Each student's paper should include a narrative section that describes in detail one example of peer pressure and group interaction. The next part of their paper should analyze how that peer pressure works for both the group and the individual member, considering the three assumptions about community around which the chapter is structured. Discourage your students from making judgments about the dynamics they uncover. Their purpose should be to objectively analyze how community expectations and values affect an individual member's behavior.

Additional Resources

Nonfiction

Caroline Knapp, *Drinking: A Love Story* (1996)   Though she began drinking seriously as a teenager, Knapp's alcoholism was largely unknown to her friends and colleagues as she attended college and began a successful career. The book also relates her struggles with anorexia to her drinking.

Alexandra Robbins, *Pledged: The Secret Life of Sororities* (2004)   Robbins went undercover in a sorority, and she details a world fraught with problems, from binge drinking to eating disorders to date rape.

Fiction

Jillian Medoff, *Hunger Point* (1997)   After losing her sister to anorexia, the narrator struggles with the reactions of her family and with her own eating disorder.

Television

Dying to Be Thin (2000)   This *NOVA* documentary addresses the general problem of anorexia and looks into the less publicized phenomena of eating disorders among men and minority women. The companion website, at http://www.pbs.org/wgbh/nova/thin/, includes streaming video of the complete program.

Richard Rodriguez, "Blaxicans" and Other Reinvented Americans (p. 120)

Using the dynamics of immigration as a starting point, Rodriguez challenges his readers to question what defines a community and to ponder how and why individuals become part of communities. As he points out, the history of American immigration has repeatedly demonstrated that members of an established community tend to resist newcomers, that those newcomers usually become part of the established community over time, and that once established, they in turn resist more recent newcomers.

Students will undoubtedly notice that Rodriguez identifies several overlapping kinds of communities in his essay: regional, linguistic, religious, and cultural among them. But central to his argument is the idea that race is itself a community and that conceptions of American racial communities were traditionally polarized between black and white until the Nixon administration added the categories of Hispanic, Native American, and Asian in the 1970s. Like Gloria Anzaldúa (see p. 53), Rodriguez rejects the notion of a monolithic Hispanic community because "there is no such thing as a Hispanic race" (par. 13). At the same time, however, he seems to accept the idea of monolithic black and white races in the United States. Why is that? You might want to explore this issue with your students: *Is* race enough to form a community on its own, or must it be combined with other factors before a functional community can emerge?

It may dismay your students to discover that Rodriguez positions race as simultaneously central and irrelevant to community formation. The key to resolving this apparent contradiction lies in his understanding of how assimilation works. As he explains it, culture is fluid (par. 17). Just as personal identities change and adapt according to circumstance and need (see chapter 1), communities—immigrant groups among them—redefine themselves as they evolve. Although a community might initially form around similarities among its members, such as racial characteristics or cultural practices, and although members may cling to their group identity for as long as possible, external influences are inevitable. When one community comes in contact with another, individual members tend to latch on to those aspects of the new community they find attractive. Each culture, in turn, adopts elements of the other. Thus, as Rodriguez puts it, "assimilation happens" (par. 17). It can't be forced or avoided. It's an organic process of creating a new community out of selected elements from other communities or cultures.

As Rodriguez sees it, racially defined communities in America are slowly, but inevitably, being displaced by culturally defined communities. As races continue to intermix, individuals are increasingly free to pick and choose among communities they most identify with, whatever their reasons.

Interrogating Assumptions

In Rodriguez's view, it is impossible for any community to sustain a stable group identity, let alone provide stability for its members. Too many external cultural factors affect a group's dynamics. Although they may strongly resist change, communities can't help but adapt to new circumstances, to redefine themselves and their members as they evolve. The very nature of community, therefore, guarantees fluidity, not stability. Furthermore, changes to the structure of an established community tend to have a strong effect on individual members' identities (par. 1) and often lead them to question who they are.

Writing about Cultural Practices

The textbook structures this as a short-term group project, and that would certainly work well as long as individual roles are clearly defined and grading criteria are structured fairly. But because this assignment touches on several of the themes covered in the book (community, identity, and tradition) and requires research, it would also work as a capstone project for an upper-level course.

However you assign it, you would do well to require students to focus on a single immigrant community. To prevent a series of reports on the same group, you may also want to assign the immigrant communities that each student group will be responsible for. Keep in mind, too, that students with immigrant backgrounds might be excited about researching their own communities. Certainly, you should encourage them to study what interests them, but avoid putting them in the position of speaking on behalf of their ethnic or racial communities.

Some students will be tempted to base all of their research on a single source, such as an encyclopedia or website. To prevent superficial accounts, require them to consult at least three sources, two of which should be primary documents. There is a wealth of source possibilities for students tackling this assignment. In addition to the local historical society and newspaper archives, they will find invaluable information in full-length book studies, genealogical resources, local and state census data, autobiographies and biographies, and published oral histories. Depending on the immigrant group they're researching, you might also encourage your students to conduct oral histories of their own by interviewing one or several immigrants or children of immigrants who live in your community.

Because of the variety of sources from which students may draw, this assignment lends itself to multimedia presentations. Students might share photographs, images of original documents (such as letters or passports), and recordings of interviews. Encourage as much creativity as students are willing to bring to the project.

Additional Resources

Nonfiction

Donald A. Ritchie, *Doing Oral History: A Practical Guide* (2003)   Ritchie explains the principles behind oral-history work and describes methods of gathering information. This resource could provide guidelines for students interested in exploring their family histories.

Ruben Martinez, *The New Americans* (2004)   In this book of essays, companion to an upcoming PBS series, Martinez looks into the lives of five immigrants. Their different backgrounds and varied lifestyles suggest the breadth of contemporary immigrant experiences in the United States.

Television

Seinfeld, "The Wizard" (1998)   Elaine tries to determine whether or not the South African immigrant she's dating is black; he believes she's Hispanic. They're each disappointed to discover that the other is white.

Web

U.S. Census Bureau, http://www.census.gov/   The Census Bureau publishes statistics on the racial makeup of the country, but the categories they use to classify people have changed often over time.

Immigration History Resource Center, http://www.ihrc.umn.edu/ Hosted by the University of Minnesota, this site contains a searchable archive of images related to immigration.

Kathleen Norris, **Can You Tell the Truth in a Small Town?** (p. 127)

Raised in New York City before she relocated to South Dakota, Kathleen Norris employs her outsider perspective to observe how the behaviors and attitudes that dominate small rural communities influence those communities and their members. Although her primary interests are the functions of history and the difficulty of writing about a community when one is immersed in it, her essay also reveals how the dynamics of small-town life can stunt both personal and community growth.

As Norris describes it, Plains communities are extraordinarily concerned with maintaining stability (see assumption 1 in the chapter introduction), even though it often comes at a cost both to individuals and to the community as a whole. Small-town traditions, established over generations, can blind people to their past by glossing over struggles, which in turn compromises their present and their future. In Lemmon, South Dakota, for example, the community's desire to "make nice," coupled with its refusal to acknowledge its arduous past, render it doubly hard to address the difficulties caused by the farm crisis of the late twentieth century. Families follow similar patterns: By romanticizing their ancestors' experiences, they allow potential conflicts to lie dormant, poised to erupt without warning or preparation. And because outsiders threaten to expose the "lies" on which traditions are built, the community remains insular and reluctant to accept new members.

Norris's observations also reveal the negative side of community-support systems. Because there are not enough people to fill every community position, each person must assume multiple roles. In serving the needs of others, therefore, an individual's needs—including privacy, autonomy, and outlets for personal growth—are often neglected. And although identity is closely tied to community, small towns like Norris's can function to overshadow or silence individual members.

Students well versed in small-town life might object to Norris's characterizations. Remind them that she writes from the perspective of someone accustomed to city life, raised to value individuality over community. She hopes that revealing uncomfortable truths will help her adopted community to grow. However, an insider's evaluation of the community would likely complicate Norris's approach. You may want to explore with your class how someone with a small-town perspective would counter (or agree with) Norris's observations.

Interrogating Assumptions

All three of the assumptions outlined in the chapter introduction factor into the attitudes of the Lemmon, South Dakota, townspeople. Foremost is the desire to establish and maintain stability. Mythologizing the past helps to create a fictional community harmony that extends itself into the present. As Norris describes it, the community does everything it can to avoid conflict and change, despite the negative effects that she sees resulting from such avoidance. The residents' willingness to assume multiple community roles demonstrates their belief that a community serves its members' needs, even as individual members complain that they don't have the time or the freedom to pursue personal goals that don't adhere to community standards. Finally, the small-town behavior Norris describes gives the lie to the notion that communities accept us for who we are. Insular rural communities like Norris's often shun newcomers and outsiders, who must adapt to the town's ways and censor themselves as much as possible if they are to have any hope of being accepted into the fold.

Writing about Cultural Practices

This assignment will be most effective if it is structured as a group oral-history project. Have each student in your class conduct one interview and share the results with the rest of the class, either as an oral presentation, a copy of the tape, or a written transcript (keep in mind that it can take from five to eight hours to transcribe one hour of tape). Students can then draw from multiple stories to write their analyses.

In addition to conducting their own oral histories, you might direct students to published collections of oral histories if any are available at a local historical society or library. Or, if the oral-history aspect seems too cumbersome, you might suggest that students consult locally written histories. They can then compare them with more traditional accounts to reach some conclusions about the functions of storytelling in community development.

However they obtain the stories that they will evaluate, students should do more in their essays than simply relate the narratives they find. Their purpose in this assignment is to consider how the stories people tell, as well as the ones they don't tell, contribute to a community's sense of what it is and how those stories address the psychological needs of a large group. Suggest to your students that approximately half of their essay's total length should be devoted to analyzing the stories they have collected.

Additional Resources

Nonfiction

Hamilton Holt, *The Life Stories of Undistinguished Americans as Told by Themselves* (1906)   Holt, editor of the newspaper the *Independent,* collected the autobiographies of working class people. The expanded edition of the book (1999) includes an introduction by Werner Sollors.

Film

Fried Green Tomatoes (1991)   An elderly woman relates a story from her youth of two women who ran the small-town Whistle Stop Cafe and the secrets they kept in order to survive.

Web

Veterans History Project, http://www.loc.gov/folklife/vets/   Sponsored by the American Folklife Center of the Library of Congress, the Veterans History Project collects firsthand accounts from World War I through the wars in Iraq and Afghanistan.

Recordings from *Division Street,* http://www.studsterkel.org/dstreet.php   For perspectives on urban life, students can listen to Studs Terkel's interviews with Chicago residents.

Small Towns, Black Lives, http://blacktowns.org/   Text and photographs from an art project on life in historically African American towns.

Maya Angelou, **Reclaiming Our Home Place** (p. 135)

In contrast to Kathleen Norris (see p. 127), Maya Angelou embraces the positive aspects of close-knit communities, especially as they are tied to place. Both writers emphasize the necessity for a community to confront its past. But whereas Norris pegs a small town's refusal to acknowledge past struggles as one cause of its current troubles, Angelou demonstrates that a determination to rectify old injustices liberates a community and helps it heal.

Students may need some background in the history of the Great Northern Migration to fully appreciate the ironies on which Angelou bases her argument. As she alludes, massive numbers of African Americans left the South after Reconstruction in a combined effort to escape Jim Crow laws that severely limited black opportunities and to aspire to a better life in the North. Between 1916 and the 1960s, more than 6 million African Americans migrated northward, usually in search of jobs in industrial cities like Chicago, Philadelphia, Detroit, St. Louis, and Cleveland. The civil rights movement of the 1960s successfully eliminated many of the conditions that inspired the migration. Beginning around 1970, more black Americans were moving to the South than were leaving it. Many of the reverse migrants were former southerners returning home, but a significant number of them had been born in the North.

Why would so many people eagerly return to a place with a history of abusing members of its community? As Angelou imagines it, home is both an instinct and a choice. Central to her argument is the idea of exile. For the most part, African Americans who left the South did so not out of choice but by necessity. The North may have held the promise of better job opportunities and perhaps more freedoms, but the South—with strong family ties, long-standing traditions, and a history of being fought for—remained home. Once the civil rights movement made the region a viable place for them to live, then, people naturally returned to it in droves. Angelou's narrative suggests that strong community ties can overcome painful pasts and geographical distances to pull people homeward, allowing them to reclaim once hostile regions as their own.

Interrogating Assumptions

Angelou builds her argument on the ideas that communities provide stability and acceptance. The South is home for many African Americans, she believes, not only because it was the home of their ancestors but also because it offers a community of people who share a history and hold similar interests. While the North may have offered (but did not necessarily deliver) better job opportunities and more freedoms, the South offers family, ancestral ties to the land, community, beauty, tradition, and memory. The concept of community support figures into Angelou's perspective as well. As long as the South subjected African Americans to slavery, segregation, and hostility, it was an unacceptable option. Once black and white southerners began to work together to address the needs of the African American community, however, the region could be reclaimed as home.

Writing about Cultural Practices

This assignment asks students to analyze a film for its cultural messages about American cities, but remind them that their focus should be on the meanings of "community." Because they'll be generalizing from a single example, stress that they must establish a narrowed thesis that can be supported with details from the film. Student efforts will be most successful if they choose a movie in which the city functions as a character in the story, rather than as merely a backdrop. To ensure that students remain focused on questions of community, consider screening a film of your choice (or one selected by student consensus) and require all of your students to use it as the basis of their analysis.

Following is a list of movies that might work well for this assignment.

Annie Hall (comedy: New York)

Batman Begins (science fiction: Gotham)

Blade Runner (science fiction: Los Angeles)

Do the Right Thing (drama: Brooklyn)

Fargo (comedy: Minneapolis)

Good Will Hunting (drama: Boston)

L.A. Story (comedy: Los Angeles)

Modern Times (comedy: New York)

Mystic River (drama: Boston)

Ocean's Eleven (drama: Las Vegas)

Saturday Night Fever (drama: New York)

Additional Resources

Nonfiction

Glenda Elizabeth Gilmore, *Gender and Jim Crow: Women and the Politics of White Supremacy in North Carolina, 1896–1920* (1996)   Gilmore explores the lives of middle class black women during one of the country's worst periods of race relations. Chapter 1, "Place and Possibility," is especially relevant.

Nicholas Lemann, *The Promised Land: The Great Black Migration and How It Changed America* (1991)   By focusing on a few individual African Americans who moved from Mississippi to Chicago, Lemann analyzes the huge social phenomenon on a personal level.

Film

The Long Walk Home (1990)   Whoopi Goldberg plays a woman struggling to raise a family during the turbulent times of the Montgomery bus boycott. Her employer (played by Sissy Spacek) only gradually becomes aware of the hardships she endures.

The Piano Lesson (1995)   Based on August Wilson's play, *The Piano Lesson* concerns a man's journey from Mississippi to Pittsburgh to reclaim a family heirloom, a piano carved with images of slavery.

Web

In Motion: The African American Migration Experience, http://www
.inmotionaame.org/migrations/landing.cfm?migration=11   The Schomberg Center for Research in Black Culture provides an overview of the great African American migrations and a collection of informative maps.

David Brooks, **Our Sprawling, Supersize Utopia** (p. 139)

Since the first families moved into Levittown, New York, in 1947, cultural critics have bemoaned the loss of community cohesiveness brought on by suburbanization. As David Brooks sees things, however, restlessness and self-imposed isolation have always been the hallmark of American identity and social behavior. Writing from a perspective deeply grounded in the thesis of Frederick Jackson Turner and in transcendental thought, Brooks describes "exurbia" as the latest frontier to promise fulfillment of the American quest for personal and social perfection.

Brooks's cultural critique draws on two central documents in American intellectual history. His idea that Americans strive for individual perfection stems directly from Ralph Waldo Emerson's seminal essay "Self-Reliance," in which the transcendentalist pleads with his peers to strive for new ideas and innovations, rather than rely on historical teachings in developing an understanding of their world. Brooks's assertion that new geographies color the American imagination is an homage to Frederick Jackson Turner's argument that the abundance of undeveloped land in North America fostered a unique American character. In the early nineteenth century, these two influences combined to inspire a rash of experimental communities—more than 100 of them were established between 1800 and 1860—in which disillusioned Americans attempted to create alternative societies that could better fulfill the promises of American exceptionalism. As Brooks interprets cultural phenomena, suburban sprawl is the late twentieth-century equivalent of the utopian impulse.

Where transcendentalists struggled to resolve the tensions between individualism and community life, Brooks suggests that communities exist solely to further the personal aspirations of their individual members. He believes that this explains why people seek out geographic enclaves of people similar to themselves and why Americans are so willing to uproot themselves in search of communities that better suit their needs. Although his essay carries a tone of optimism and staunch defense of American suburbia, challenge your students to question his characterizations of late twentieth-century communities. Many will take issue with his stereotypes of some groups, while others may not be convinced by his assertions that American materialism is a positive force. In debating whether Brooks successfully counters the prevailing criticisms of suburban sprawl, remind your students to consider opposing ideas about the functions of community. To complicate your students' perspectives on suburban and rural utopias, consider referring them to Hostetler's essay about the Amish (p. 99) and Kathleen Norris's examination of the dynamics of small-town living (p. 127).

Interrogating Assumptions

Brooks's glowing assessment of the opportunities inherent in suburban sprawl rests on two assumptions: that communities exist to serve individuals' needs (assumption 2) and that people are free to pick and choose among narrowly defined communities in search of those that best suit them (assumption 3). Stability (assumption 1) is the furthest thing from Brooks's mind. For him, the beauty of American culture lies in its never-ending quest for something better.

Writing about Cultural Practices

Both of the writing projects that accompany Brooks's essay encourage students to apply his argument to their own experiences. The first assignment calls for a personal essay that tests Brooks's thesis. Rather than simply agreeing with or disputing Brooks's assertions, writers should narrate their personal accounts in detail and be careful to articulate *why* they respond to his points the way they do. Encourage them, as well, to offer alternative explanations for American mobility. For an example of a personal narrative that offers an opposing perspective on the drive behind internal migration, refer your students to Maya Angelou's "Reclaiming Our Home Place" on page 135.

The second assignment requires students to critically analyze the symbolic meanings of a cultural artifact. They will have more success if they choose an object, whether private or public, that carries personal resonance. Explain to them that the subject of their analysis does not have to be new. Some of the most compelling symbols of forward thinking may well be found among family heirlooms or historic landmarks. Students might consult family or community members to assess what meanings the object holds for others; they should also consider how they respond to it themselves. Whatever your students choose to write about, stress that they will need to look beyond the object's practical functions and contemplate what additional, perhaps subconscious, meanings it holds for the people who use it.

Additional Resources

Nonfiction

Ralph Waldo Emerson, "Self-Reliance" (1841)   Emerson's essays, particularly "Self-Reliance," form a foundation for American utopian movements. The essays are collected in a volume edited by Alfred R. Ferguson and Jean Ferguson Carr (1987).

Fiction

Sinclair Lewis, *Babbitt* (1922)   George F. Babbitt is the center around which Sinclair Lewis forms a critique of the hypocrisy in middle class life.

Television

Desperate Housewives   The show's tagline, "All is not as it seems on Wisteria Lane," hints at the secrets behind these housewives' flawless facades.

Web

Brook Farm, http://www.transcendentalists.com/brook_farm.htm   A history of Brook Farm, a utopian experiment that grew out of the transcendentalist movement.

Andrew Leonard, **You Are Who You Know** (p. 150)
Jennifer Bishop Fulwiler, **An Ode to Friendster** (p. 156)

If you're not familiar with Friendster and networks like it, spend some time exploring it to get a sense of the virtual community that many of your students likely belong to. Then, before discussing the readings paired here, poll your class about their use of online social networking. Do they and their friends, as Leonard argues, count on networks like Friendster to hook them up with other people who might be able to fulfill their personal desires (friendship, romance, employment, something to do)? Are the sites a source of entertainment, as Fulwiler suggests? Is there some middle ground? The most important question to pose to your students, however, might be whether they think of online networks as communities, and why they answer the way they do.

Since the Internet came into widespread use, and even before, pundits and scholars have debated its effects on social interaction. Some argue that the easy connectivity it provides enhances offline communities; others fret that it fosters isolation while creating the illusion of connection. The readings reprinted here continue the ongoing debate. The writers are critical of the many online social networks that have gained massive popularity in the past few years, yet both participate in them. A specialist in technology and culture, Andrew Leonard cautions that the data-saturated networks are as attractive to marketers and researchers as they are to their members. Jennifer Bishop Fulwiler, on the other hand, is fully enamored of Friendster—not, it would seem, because it can link her up with people who may be able to help her pursue a goal, but because it's a source of endless fascination. More to the point, Leonard and Fulwiler are critical of these virtual communities precisely because they question their authenticity as communities. Although online social networks may promise interpersonal connections, those connections are "flimsy," tenuous, and inherently suspect.

Both articles raise some of the central assumptions about community outlined in the chapter introduction. Networking sites promise to help their members locate and connect with hundreds of other people who share similar interests (assumption 1), but Leonard questions the usefulness of such connections, and Fulwiler is surprised to discover that her friends' friends seem so freakish to her. Services like Friendster also promise that virtual networking with thrice-removed acquaintances will serve members' social needs (assumption 2), but Leonard points out that by willingly broadcasting personal information to millions of strangers, participants put themselves at risk of being monitored, or worse. And as Fulwiler and Leonard both caution, most online "friends" don't really know each other very well at all (assumption 3). Any community they might form, therefore, seems superficial at best.

The Friendster phenomenon is still in its infancy. Despite their critical stances, both Leonard and Fulwiler derive some satisfaction from their online social networks, and both implicitly hold out hope that a real sense of community might emerge from their involvement. Referring back to the assumptions that underpin contemporary ideas about community, explore with your students whether such a possibility exists.

Interrogating Assumptions

Leonard's and Fulwiler's opposing attitudes about the "flimsiness" of online networking connections stem from their differing assumptions about the values of online communities. For Leonard, the promise of electronic social networking lies in its opportunities for advancing individual needs: He approaches Friendster, Orkut, and similar services as something comparable to traditional "old boys' networks." Their purpose, for him, is to produce "weak ties" and "fresh territory" that can widen a person's search for occupational and romantic leads. He does not expect to develop close friendships online and so is not disappointed that they don't emerge. Fulwiler, on the other hand, is searching for a supportive community of like-minded people who accept each other for who they are. As she sees it, the superficiality of the profile system renders it impossible to really know any of the "friends" one might collect online, and so she is frustrated that the sites can't deliver on what she interprets as their promise.

Writing about Cultural Practices

Students do not need any programming or HTML experience to tackle this assignment successfully. Their purpose is not to create an actual site but to imagine one. They should start by analyzing the structures of at least two existing social-networking sites: Friendster.com, Orkut.com, ZeroDegrees.com, Tribe .net, LinkedIn.com, or MySpace.com, for example. (Many of these sites require registration before allowing a person to enter. Remind your students that they can create free, temporary email addresses with services such as Hotmail and Yahoo!) As students observe and analyze these websites, they will begin forming their own critical perspectives on how such sites create (or don't) a sense of community for their users. This exercise will help students begin to articulate the principles of, or assumptions about, what makes a community that they, in turn, will use to create an alternative social-networking site.

How students outline their proposed site will depend on their preferred methods of brainstorming and organizing information. Encourage your students to use whatever strategies work best for them. Some may want to use a traditional outline; some may want to create a relationship tree; some may be more comfortable using clusters; some may prefer prose description; others may try a storyboard format; computer-savvy students may even be eager to create sample webpages. If any students object to the computer access requirements of the assignment, allow them the option of creating an offline network, such as a social club or a yearbook. Remind all of your students that although they should be creative and thorough in imagining their own websites, the core of this assignment is their written analysis of community development and a thoughtful explanation of how their social network would facilitate it.

Additional Resources

Film

You've Got Mail (1998)   Though it seems dated now, this Tom Hanks/Meg Ryan comedy was one of the first movies to deal with a computer-mediated relationship.

Must Love Dogs (2005)   A newer take on online matches, *Must Love Dogs* stars Diane Lane and John Cusack as a couple who meet through a dating site.

Television

Hooking Up   This reality show looks into the world of online dating, featuring 11 women who try to find love over the Internet.

Web

Myspace, http://www.myspace.com/   Myspace, which allows users to create their own blogs and emphasizes communities based on musical interests, is already eclipsing Friendster as *the* place to meet online.

Meetup, http://www.meetup.com   A hybrid of online and real-world networking, Meetup allows users to find others in their area with similar interests with the goal of arranging group meetings.

Bill Donahue and Peter Granser, **The Land of the Setting Sun** (p. 161)

American culture has long neglected the senior community, assuming that elders are inactive and have little to contribute to society. As nearly 80 million baby boomers (those born between 1946 and 1964) move into retirement age, over-55 communities have grown increasingly popular. These planned neighborhoods of condominiums, townhouses, and single-family homes, which typically restrict membership to older singles and couples, cater to an updated senior lifestyle. Rejecting the decades-old concept of the retirement home, in which warehoused residents are generally assumed to sit around quietly and do little but play cards, retirement communities provide assistance for the tasks of daily living while offering several recreational and community-building activities for their active members.

These images of life in Sun City simultaneously embrace and undermine popular stereotypes of retirement. Bill Donahue suggests that this is a community in which nature and decay are kept under strict control, a subversive attempt by the residents to counter or ignore their own aging processes. But the images belie his contention. The landscape is neat, orderly, and disarmingly artificial (consider the flock of plastic flamingos and the perfectly manicured shrubbery), but it exudes an undercurrent of playfulness. The residents of Sun City look as though they're enjoying a permanent vacation. Smiling as they soak up the Arizona sun, they all appear to be casually relaxed. Even the artificial dog sports a mischievous grin.

Students may notice that the people in these photographs are a racially and ethnically homogenous group. You may want to explore whether their similarities suggest something insidious about planned communities. Encourage your students to draw parallels between this self-segregated community and the ethnic enclaves of urban environments. Have these seniors chosen to surround themselves with like-minded peers, or have they insulated themselves from an indifferent culture that excludes them from participating in mainstream social life? Donahue rejects arguments that seniors drawn to over-55 neighborhoods should instead integrate themselves with mixed-age communities; clearly the residents of Sun City do as well. Ask your students to ponder what retirement communities offer that more diverse communities cannot. What do the residents gain by relocating? What do they lose?

This photo essay begs to be studied in connection with David Brooks's essay "Our Sprawling, Supersize Utopia" (p. 139), which argues that the explosion of narrowly defined suburban and exurban communities such as Sun City, far from exemplifying conformity or lack of imagination, reflects an American impulse to look to the future while seeking perfection. The American dream, as he describes it, is a longing for a paradise that is just around the corner. Explore with your students how the residents of Sun City epitomize what Brooks calls the "Paradise Spell." Rather than remain in communities that they may have been part of for decades, the residents of Sun City packed everything up and relocated to share their retirement years with people very much like them. Are they looking to an imagined future happiness, or have they finally attained it?

Interrogating Assumptions

These images depict a community devoid of age-based hierarchy. In some parts of the world, the elderly are revered. They are the heads of the household, the family decision makers, and often have the last word. In America, by contrast, communities like Sun City emerge because of the inherent invisibility the elderly face in the culture. So, for better or worse, in a community whose very foundation is the age of its members, there is a homogeneity that extends far beyond race, wealth, political affiliation, and the like. New systems of hierarchy must surface and rely on less traditional means.

Writing about Cultural Practices

This assignment asks for a cognitive leap that may at first cause students to throw up their hands in frustration. In order to draw a workable comparison between simulated communities and planned communities, they will need to deconstruct both types in an effort to identify the elements that their founders used to build them. Send them to Del Webb Corporation's website to find the developer's explanations of how its retirement communities are planned and constructed and how they function. If your students have played games like SimCity or SimLife, they should be able to figure out pretty readily what elements the game developers determined form the building blocks of community. If they are unfamiliar with the genre, however, the task will require you to provide more instructional support.

Additional Resources

Nonfiction

Hubert Stroud, *The Promise of Paradise: Recreational and Retirement Communities in the United States since 1950* (2001)   Stroud examines the growth of retirement communities in the United States, focusing on their geographical features and environmental impacts.

Television

The Golden Girls   Four single older women, with four contrasting personalities, share a home in Miami Beach.

Web

Aging Hipsters, http://www.aginghipsters.com/   This site, which hints at an online retirement community, provides news and discussion for the baby-boomer generation.

American Association of Retired Persons, http://www.aarp.org/   AARP's website has a section on housing choices that surveys options for retirees.

Del Webb Corporation, http://www.delwebb.com   The site of the company that developed Sun City features a biography of founder Del Webb, a pioneer of planned communities.

Mixing Words and Images:
Picturing Communities (p. 169)

Most of your students will likely be unfamiliar with the photo essay genre. Before you set them to work on this assignment, therefore, spend some time with them analyzing a few of the photo essays included in *ReMix*. Within chapter 2, you might examine Bill Donahue and Peter Granser's "The Land of the Setting Sun" (p. 161) as well as the Westside Alternative High School images that introduce the assignment. Other photo essays in the book include "When I Grow Up" (p. 12), Celia A. Shapiro's "Last Suppers" (p. 198), and John Margolies's "Amazing! Incredible! The Roadside Attraction" (p. 398). Ask students to discuss how the text and images complement each other, how the photographs are used to advance an argument, and what would be lost if either element were removed.

As they prepare to take their pictures, stress to your students that their photographs will be not illustrations of a written argument, but rather an integral part of the argument itself. Just as writers often don't know what they want to say until they try to express themselves in words, photographers often discover the purpose of their photographs only after they see what they've captured with their lens. With this in mind, encourage your students to take many more pictures than they think they need (at least 15 or 20) and to leave themselves enough time to go back and take more after they have begun to put their thoughts together. If they're using film photography, remind them to leave time (and budget) for development. Access to a digital camera and familiarity with the "insert pictures" and "text box" functions of word-processing programs will simplify the composition aspect of this assignment, but don't require technical sophistication from your students unless you're reasonably certain that it won't hinder their creative and argumentative progress.

Connecting to Culture: Suggestions for Writing (p. 170)

The writing assignments that conclude the chapter offer students an opportunity to synthesize the ideas they've encountered in the readings, to consider their own experiences in light of what they've read, and to make some conclusions about the assumptions outlined in the chapter introduction.

Network Connections: Mapping Your Social Identity

This project encourages students to test ideas from the chapter by applying them to their personal experiences—specifically, by examining their social networks and assessing how multiple interpersonal relationships affect their sense of who they are. Because the assignment relies so heavily on an understanding of identity, it is best assigned in conjunction with, or following, an exploration of the readings in chapter 1. There are several productive techniques students might use to create their maps. For some, clustering will come naturally. Others may prefer something resembling a family tree; still others may want to experiment with a photo collage. Also useful would be an outline. Whatever method your students use to map their social networks, make sure they understand that it is only the starting point for the project. Once they have a visual image of their personal communities, they'll need to evaluate how those communities function together (and separately) to shape their identity.

Reality Check: Evaluating Virtual Communities

This assignment combines online research and close analysis of a single example to advance an argument about the ideas students have encountered in their reading. Start by pointing out to your class that they need not rely solely on those readings that examine virtual communities (those by Mim Udovitch, Andrew Leonard, and Jennifer Bishop Fulwiler): Any of the essays and images they've examined will provide insights that they can apply to a specific online community. Before drafting their papers, students should spend some time over several days observing or participating in the online community of their choice. Good resources for finding virtual communities include Google Groups and Yahoo!'s directory service; students might also ask friends and family members if they belong to any online groups. Although not necessary, they might consider posting a question in the community's forum, asking what the members view to be the purposes of the group and whether they themselves think of it as a community. Their final papers should include the student's definition of "community," with a description of the qualities and characteristics of a community; a narrative description of the virtual community they investigated; and a well-supported argument either for or against considering that particular group as a "real" community.

Interrogating Assumptions: How Do Communities Function?

The most formal of the writing projects in this chapter, this final assignment calls for a text-based comparative analysis that synthesizes ideas from the chapter and several individual readings. Encourage students to select readings that are closely related thematically as well as in the manner they address assumptions about community. If you've assigned or discussed any of the Interrogating Assumptions or Connecting to Another Reading questions that follow some of the selections in the chapter, encourage students to use their responses as starting points for their drafts. A successful student essay will posit a thesis about one of the assumptions and use the readings to support it, rather than simply compare and contrast several selections.

3 Tradition

. . . or, why would you eat <u>that</u>?

Although we all participate in a myriad of traditions throughout the course of our lives, we may take them for granted. We may rarely question their origins or their purposes—or how they influence our thinking and behavior. An old joke illustrates how ingrained traditions can become. As the story goes, a young bride cuts a roast in half as she prepares to cook it, prompting her husband to ask why. She answers that her mother always did it that way. Curious, she in turn asks her mother why she cuts her roasts in half and receives the same answer she gave her husband: That's how mom always did it. Not satisfied with the response, the newlyweds decide to pose the question to the grandmother: Why did you cut your roasts in half before cooking them? Well, she tells them, I didn't own a pan big enough to hold a whole roast. This anecdote illustrates two important points. First, many traditions started out as practices that often did not have deep meaning or significance, and second, regardless of the fact of their origins, traditions have the power to bond people across generations.

Even if they have never thought about how tradition affects them, each of your students should be able to identify at least one ritual that has an important role in his or her life, whether it's something as formal as a religious ceremony or as recreational as a weekly game of poker with friends. Before you have them read the chapter introduction, you may want to explore, as a class or as a preliminary journal assignment, what assumptions your students currently hold about tradition. Brainstorm as a group what constitutes a tradition and, based on the class's preliminary definition of "tradition," try to identify several examples that your students are familiar with. Who participates in these traditions? When and why did they start? What do they mean? How have they changed? Why are they important?

As they work through the chapter, students will examine different conceptions of how traditions emerge, what traditions reveal about those who participate in them, and how traditions function in contemporary society. The Examining the Everyday activity that opens the chapter encourages students to take an initial step in that direction, asking them to base their interpretations on a popular food associated with their hometowns or current communities.

If possible, try to time your teaching of this chapter to coincide with a major national or local holiday or event. Thanksgiving is an obvious choice, but a cultural fair or an annual campus festival would work equally well. Like the Examining the Everyday project, several of the assignments that accompany the readings or conclude the chapter ask students to observe and analyze a local tradition. Having access to one or more events scheduled nearby will simplify your efforts and intensify students' engagement with the chapter's theme.

Because the central assumptions outlined in the chapter's introduction form the basis for analyzing the chapter's readings, spend some time discussing them in class. Use the questions that follow each discussion of an assumption to explore the concept with your students. You may want to ask your students whether they agree or disagree with the outlined assumptions and to identify other assumptions about tradition. Discuss with your class, also, how these assumptions function in American culture: Who holds them? What purposes do they serve? Are they helpful or harmful? And how do students see them played out in their personal lives and in the world around them?

All of the chapter's readings explore one or several of the three main assumptions outlined in the introduction—traditions are long-standing and static practices; traditions always preserve an authentic version of the past; and traditions promote unity. As the chapter subtitle suggests, a culinary theme runs through the chapter. Several readings explore rituals surrounding food and eating: In "Thoroughly Modern Dining" (p. 188), Richard Pillsbury considers the cultural implications of the increasing preference for eating celebratory meals in restaurants rather than preparing them at home; Charles Bowden's essay "Last Meals and the People Who Eat Them" (p. 195) and Celia A. Shapiro's photo exhibit "Last Suppers" (p. 198) examine the cultural meanings behind condemned prisoners' final meals; and Garrison Keillor shares a telling and humorous story about a family Thanksgiving in "A Wobegon Holiday Dinner" (p. 225). Counter-traditions are another recurring theme: Ana Castillo, Jenn Shreve, and Gamaliel Padilla examine how new traditions emerge, with considerations of family bedtime conventions, mourning rituals, and etiquette, respectively. Four of the readings investigate the origins of long-standing traditions and contemplate their meanings: Jon Stewart pokes fun at the clichéd themes of commencement addresses, David Berreby and Laura Randall explore the social and political implications of campus rituals, and Ayana D. Byrd and Lori L. Tharps explain the cultural significance of hair rituals. Finally, two readings explore symbols of patriotism and American identity: Brent Staples offers an original interpretation of American flags and hard hats, while Natalie Guice Adams and Pamela J. Bettis argue that the practice of cheerleading invokes both the best and the worst traits typically ascribed to Americans.

Additional Resources

Nonfiction

Eric Hobsbawm and Terence Ranger, *The Invention of Tradition* (1983)
Hobsbawn and Ranger expose the relatively recent origins of traditions
many people take to be much longer established, focusing on British royal
and imperial rituals.

Fiction

Robert Olen Butler, *A Good Scent from a Strange Mountain* (1992) Butler's
Pulitzer Prize–winning short-story collection focuses on a Vietnamese community in New Orleans. His characters struggle to maintain their folklore
and traditions as they adjust to life in America.

Film

Indian Summer (1993) A group of adults return to their childhood summer
camp to relive some of its traditions before it closes its final season.

Ana Castillo, **Bowing Out** (p. 185)

This brief personal narrative offers a compelling look at how people invent traditions to cope with change as they sort out their interpersonal relationships.
Castillo focuses on a bedtime tradition that her son established when he entered
puberty—a time of awkward maturation and confusion about identity. Rather
than gather cues from his own heritage, Marcel borrows a tradition from a culture to which he has no connection and turns it into something of his own, with
specific meanings for him and his mother.

Those meanings are intensely personal yet also somewhat universal. Castillo
describes her son's bow and formalized language as "an elegant ritual of respect
toward his mother" (par. 1). What they mean to Marcel we can never be sure, but
Castillo suggests that it's a way for him to establish a mature distance from his
mother while maintaining a close familial bond. Using a language she doesn't
understand further establishes his growing independence; in making a ritual of
it, however, he simultaneously includes his mother in his emerging adult identity. At this transitional point in their relationship, mother and son establish a
tradition that helps them hold on to their past connections even as they venture
into new territory.

Interrogating Assumptions

In Castillo's case, family traditions are more about forging bonds and negotiating change than they are about honoring the past. Although nearly everything

between mother and son is undergoing transition, Marcel's invented ritual establishes continuity and helps to restructure their relationship as he matures.

Writing about Cultural Practices

Especially this early in their progress with the chapter, your students may have difficulty identifying family traditions that aren't associated with major holidays. For the assignment to work, however, you will need to strongly discourage them from writing about the obvious contenders: Thanksgiving, religious celebrations, Independence Day, Memorial Day, and Labor Day. To help them conceive of minor rituals as traditions, encourage students to share some ideas in class, letting their classmates steer them away from clichés and toward something more fruitful. Point them to Castillo's essay for examples. The traditions she describes include not only her son's formal bow but also their "predictable" comments, their combined candor and reticence, her bedtime activities, the dog's wariness, and her status as an unmarried adult.

At the same time, remember that family interactions can be as difficult as they can be pleasant. There is a chance that this assignment will provoke memories that students may not want to expose. To lower the stakes, consider offering this topic as a journal assignment that you will read but will refrain from commenting on in class.

Additional Resources

Nonfiction

Dave Lowry, *Traditions: Essays on the Japanese Martial Arts and Ways* (2002)   In these essays, Lowry explicates martial arts customs, including the bow.

Patricia Stevens, *Between Mothers and Sons: Women Writers Talk about Having Sons and Raising Men* (1999)   In this collection of short stories and essays, mothers contemplate the emotional ties they form with their sons and how these relationships are sometimes complicated by adolescence.

Film

Some Mother's Son (1996)   Set against the backdrop of a hunger strike by Northern Irish prisoners, this movie focuses on two mothers. Despite their differing politics, they form an alliance to try to save their sons' lives.

Richard Pillsbury, **Thoroughly Modern Dining** (p. 188)

Embracing a nostalgic view of the meaning and function of family meals, food historian Richard Pillsbury bemoans the loss of a tradition that has been very important in his life but that appears to be waning: the home-cooked celebration dinner. As he sees it, elaborate meals shared over the family table bonded relatives across generations and assured that every family member would feel both special and connected to something larger. As this tradition is being supplanted by restaurant outings, Pillsbury fears no less than the dissolution of the nuclear family.

Students may not immediately recognize that Pillsbury's argument rests on two widely disputed assumptions. According to his view, family-cooked meals lovingly prepared by a mother for her husband, children, and extended family were standard fare among American families until the late twentieth century. He further asserts that the arduous task of cooking and providing these meals was a cherished way for women to play the role of "the dispenser of personalized love and attention" (par. 9). But in reality, the "traditional" nuclear group of married stay-at-home mother and working father with two or more children never represented the majority of American families, and many women who served the role of homemaker in the middle of the century would dispute Pillsbury's romanticized picture of the selfless mother, happily toiling away in the kitchen. Although Pillsbury hints at the gender inequities and cultural priorities that relegated women to the domestic sphere until very recently, he dismisses the possibility that his golden age of family dining might have been oppressive to "the ranking cook in the household." And although he recognizes that the newer tradition reflects changing values and might indeed be better for the women of a family, Pillsbury concludes by implying that abandoning the family kitchen may lead to irreparable social and cultural harm.

For students born at the tail end of the twentieth century, the restaurant celebration may be the only tradition they know, and Pillsbury's traditional scenario might well be a foreign concept to them. With this in mind, consider opening class discussion by polling your students about their experiences with family meals: Who celebrates at home, and who goes out? What did their parents' families do? Ask them if Pillsbury's descriptions ring true and whether they sense anything missing from his argument. Your class might quickly discover that the custom Pillsbury longs for is far from universal. What, then, do they make of his argument? How does its effectiveness, in turn, influence his predictions?

For an amusing personal narrative that counters Pillsbury's thesis, see Garrison Keillor's "A Wobegon Holiday Dinner," on page 225.

Interrogating Assumptions

Pillsbury would reject the idea that traditions are static and long-standing. As he points out, old traditions are supplanted by new ones, and the changes can take place swiftly. Since he acknowledges that he and his brother have differing memories and interpretations of their shared family meals, and considering his overview of the history of restaurants, he might dispute the notion that traditions preserve an authentic version of the past. All the same, he clings to tradition in an effort to maintain a way of life that's important to him.

Writing about Cultural Practices

Once they get started, most students will likely enjoy this project, which encourages them to take a fresh look at a cultural environment they may have taken for granted. They might not be accustomed to practicing close observation and critical reading of a physical space, but it should come rather naturally. With the assignment's analytic angle in hand, many will be at first surprised by what they find, then increasingly excited by their discoveries.

Visiting the restaurant they write about will be eye opening and valuable for students, but they should be able to manage effective papers without the pressure to blow their budgets on potato skins and baby back ribs. Even if they cannot physically examine the space, there are several resources available for them to study. Print, television, and radio advertisements are essential, of course, as is any Web presence the restaurant may have. Students might try to obtain a copy of the restaurant's description from its menus. It may also be useful for them to obtain and study the opening pages of the restaurant's annual report, assuming the chain is publicly held. Not only will a shareholder's report summarize the chain's theme and financial results, but in many cases it will also express the restaurant's philosophy, goals, and strategies for drawing in new and repeat customers. It might even analyze which strategies were most effective. Public companies will mail their annual reports for free on request; many make them available for download on the corporate website.

The most difficult part of this project for students could be organizing all of the information they gather. Students might borrow Pillsbury's technique of beginning with a straight narrative description of their subject before delving into analysis, but some will be more comfortable opening with their thesis statement and proceeding from there. Comparing and contrasting home and restaurant experiences could also be an effective approach. Because they're writing about a place, you may want to review spatial organization with them. You might also suggest that they incorporate visuals—photos, maps of floor plans, and so on—in their analyses.

Additional Resources

Nonfiction

Stephanie Coontz, *The Way We Never Were* (1992)   Coontz calls into question the prototype of the American nuclear family, debunking popular ideas about how "normal" families were in the 1950s.

Susan Marks, *Finding Betty Crocker: The Secret Life of America's First Lady of Food* (2005)   There was no real Betty Crocker, so General Mills had to invent (and reinvent) her. Marks traces the changing image of the trademark.

Film

Eat Drink Man Woman (1994)   A chef and his three daughters come together each week for a traditional meal, which binds them to one another through times of change.

PAIRED READINGS: FOCUS ON LAST MEALS

Charles Bowden, **Last Meals and the People Who Eat Them** (p. 195)
Celia A. Shapiro, **Last Suppers** (p. 198)

Bowden's essay and Shapiro's photographs raise questions that have no clear or easy answers. Why are special last meals served to those about to be executed? Why are witnesses to the execution treated to a buffet? Why allow steaks and ice cream for the condemned but not liquor, cigarettes, nor a last evening with a loved one? As you prepare to tackle these questions in class, keep in mind that your students will hold a variety of positions on the death penalty. They will quickly catch on that Charles Bowden is vehemently opposed to executions, but it may take them longer to determine Shapiro's stance. Because the death penalty is such a contentious issue, there is a real risk that discussion of this photo essay could devolve into an angry debate. To avoid an unproductive class period, do what you can to focus students on the "traditions" surrounding prisoners' last meals and what those traditions suggest both about American values and about the people who are sentenced to death.

This can be accomplished by taking a formalistic approach to Bowden's text and Shapiro's photographs. Examine the writer's allusions and the artist's compositions. Bowden, for example, invokes historic traditions surrounding ritual sacrifice, last meals, and executions, speculating that contemporary practice derives from ancient custom—possibly Christian, Jewish, or Greek. By linking a modern practice many consider barbaric to iconic models of civilized cultures,

Bowden suggests, the prison custom implicitly asserts that the executions are a civilized practice sanctioned by generations of our ancestors. Draw your students' attention, in particular, to the title of Shapiro's photo exhibit. "Last Suppers" is a direct reference to Christian tradition. As the story goes, Jesus of Nazareth and his twelve apostles shared a final meal the evening before Christ's crucifixion. During this meal, Jesus predicted, rightly, that one of his followers would betray him. Although your students may or may not have been raised in the Christian tradition, Shapiro's reference to the story attaches similar themes—hypocrisy, betrayal, forgiveness—to the subjects of her photographs.

At the same time, Shapiro's photographs attempt to subvert a penal tradition by subverting an artistic tradition: the still-life genre, the earliest examples of which were used to celebrate wealth and consumption. The stark simplicity of the meals she portrays manages to raise serious questions about the practice of state-sanctioned execution while underscoring the disadvantaged social class of those executed. Although the viewer knows that the people who chose these meals were convicted of horrific acts of violence, somehow a box of children's cereal or a dozen hot dogs humanizes the condemned and makes them sympathetic, if not difficult to imagine as threats to society. And the knowledge that these meals are a precursor to death adds its own level of horror for those who view them.

Writing about Cultural Practices

Most of your students will likely be unfamiliar with the photo essay genre. Before you set them to work on this assignment, therefore, spend some time with them analyzing a few of the photo essays included in *ReMix*. In addition to Bowden's and Shapiro's work on prisoners' last meals, you might examine Bill Donahue and Peter Granser's "The Land of the Setting Sun" (p. 161), the Westside Alternative High School images (p. 168), "When I Grow Up" (p. 12), and John Margolies's "Amazing! Incredible! The Roadside Attraction" (p. 398). Ask students to discuss how the text and images complement each other, how the photographs are used to advance an argument, and what would be lost if either element were removed.

As they prepare to take their pictures, stress to your students that their photographs will be not illustrations of a written analysis, but an integral part of the analysis itself. Just as writers often don't know what they want to say until they try to express themselves in words, photographers often discover the purpose of their photographs only after they see what they've captured with their lens. With this in mind, encourage your students to take many more pictures than they think they need (at least 15 or 20) and to leave themselves enough time to go back and take more after they have begun to put their thoughts together. If they're using film photography, remind them to leave time (and budget) for development. Access to a digital camera and familiarity with the "insert pictures" and "text box" functions of word-processing programs will simplify the composition aspect of this assignment, but don't require technical sophistication from your students unless you're reasonably certain that it won't hinder their creative and argumentative progress.

Additional Resources

Nonfiction

Brian Price, *Meals to Die For* (2004)   A former prison cook describes how he grudgingly became the preparer of last meals.

Web

Last Supper and *The Big Feed,* http://www.uks.no/uksforum/arkiv/3499/ html/videos.html   Streaming video is available on this site of two documentaries that examine the origins of the last-meal tradition.

The Memory Hole, http://www.thememoryhole.org/deaths/ texas-final-meals.htm   This list of prisoners' last meals used to be posted on the Texas Department of Criminal Justice website.

Jon Stewart, **Commencement Address** (p. 201)

Even though your students may not have attended many graduations, they should be able to cull from Stewart's satirical speech a reasonably complete catalog of the overworn clichés of the commencement address. You might want to have the class review his speech paragraph by paragraph, identifying the various themes he turns upside down, or you might simply ask your students to name some of the themes they recognized and gather their responses on the board. Among the traditional themes Stewart invokes are hard work, possibility, responsibility, success, progress, social justice, the "real world," memories, maturity, wisdom, and honor—cornerstone American values. Although he satirizes these themes ruthlessly at times, the fact remains that they serve as the foundation for his address; Stewart is continuing the tradition even as he mocks it.

Work with your class to explore why these themes are so pervasive at high school and college graduation ceremonies. Graduation, or commencement, is a time of roiling emotions for its attendees. Graduating students and their families experience pride, relief, nostalgia, excitement, and anxiety, often all at once. Ritualized behaviors can develop and continue as a way to manage these emotions. Commencement speeches do this, partly, by connecting the graduates to the students who have come before them and will come after them. Remind your students that the alma mater is a significant community for many college graduates, who identify with a large group of peers and who tap into its network of fellow graduates for support, advice, and personal advancement. The traditional rituals of the commencement ceremony function to formally initiate new graduates into that community.

Writing about Cultural Practices

Formally analyzing the elements of a successful speech or piece of writing is an excellent method for emerging writers to learn what contributes to effective composition. You may need to explain to your students what a rhetorical analysis is and how to construct one. Stress that their purpose in this assignment is to analyze a speech, not respond to its themes. They should examine how the speechwriter uses language and structure to make his or her points. Among the characteristics students might look for are word choice, repeated elements, literary devices such as metaphor and irony, organization, and syntax.

Students should also consider the audience for the speech, the speechwriter's purpose, and the cultural context in which the address was given. They may not know that commencement addresses are a popular vehicle for public figures to advance larger political and social arguments or that some of the most significant documents in American intellectual and political history were drafted as commencement addresses. Here, Jon Stewart uses his address to the graduating class of the College of William and Mary to criticize the Bush administration and to protest the war in Iraq. As students prepare their analyses, therefore, encourage them to research the current events that were taking place at the time the speech was delivered. Knowing what the speaker is responding to will help them construct more effective analyses.

Additional Resources

Nonfiction

John William McCluskey, *The Complete Book of Wedding Toasts* (2001)   Like commencement speeches, toasts follow given forms and traditions. This book provides a number of "genuine" sentiments from which to choose.

Web

"Advice, Like Youth, Probably Wasted on the Young," http://www .chicagotribune.com/news/columnists/chi-970601sunscreen,0,4664776. column   Mary Schmich's now-famous advice to graduates, with its admonition to "wear sunscreen," was published in the Chicago *Tribune.*

American University Commencement Address, http://www.americanrhetoric .com/speeches/jfkamericanuniversityaddress.html   In John F. Kennedy's historic speech at American University, he announces a nuclear test-ban treaty with the Soviet Union. A transcript and audio file are available on the American Rhetoric site.

David Berreby, **It Takes a Tribe** (p. 207)
Laura Randall, **Things You Only Do in College** (p. 211)

Originally published as a feature article (Berreby) and a sidebar (Randall), these two essays work well together because Randall's examples illustrate the kinds of traditional rituals that Berreby asserts are integral to establishing community identity. Berreby builds his cultural critique on the findings of several related but independent studies from a number of competing disciplines. Spend some time reviewing the studies he cites and discussing their findings. Ask your students to explain how Berreby synthesizes the research to reach his own conclusions, and ask whether they are convinced by his argument. Does their own experience support his thesis or contradict it?

The college campus is a fascinating laboratory for studying how people attach themselves to narrowly defined communities. As Berreby points out, college affiliations—and the subaffiliations they spawn—can be exceedingly arbitrary, yet people consistently latch on quickly and permanently. Consider making a laboratory of your own classroom. Poll your students to determine what group affiliations they represent and how strongly they feel about their microcommunities. Even better, consider reproducing one of the studies Berreby cites in his article. First, have your students name several different formal and informal groups on campus, and then have them rank those groups according to how well they qualify as communities. (This experiment will be more effective if you haven't already worked through the chapter on community.) After the class has established a hierarchy, put each group on the board in ascending order of rank and ask students to identify any rituals and traditions these groups practice. With any luck, your students will see a direct correlation between the amount of involvement required by group membership and where that group ranks in their hierarchy.

After you've worked with the class to enhance their understanding of how seemingly harmless rituals can foster an "us-versus-them" mentality, devote time to exploring the implications of Berreby's findings. He limits his focus to college life and academics (while cleverly playing disciplinary rivalries off each other) but argues that the studies' findings suggest that tribal thinking can have serious sociopolitical consequences. Encourage your students to pick up Berreby's argument where he leaves off. Where, outside of the college and university setting, do they see rituals used to cement group allegiance? What consequences have they witnessed? And finally, is Berreby justified in suggesting that hazing and genocide stem from the same cultural impulses?

Interrogating Assumptions

As Berreby explains it, even historically meaningless rituals are important because they play an active role in establishing unity and cementing group loyalty. Rituals can manufacture surprisingly strong community identities even when there are no historic or interpersonal criteria for establishing belonging. What's more, participating in invented traditions fosters a sense of superiority for a group's members, a feeling "that an essential trait separates them from the rest of humanity" (par. 5). People feel such a profound "need to belong, to feel a part of 'us' " (8), that they will happily ignore the lack of a strong cultural or historic foundation for group membership, just as long as they can get in. And the more effort, or "sweat, tears, and embarrassment" (20), required to join, the more significant the community affiliation is to a person's identity and loyalty to the group, regardless of how meaningless the group may actually be.

Writing about Cultural Practices

This assignment invites students to adopt the role of cultural anthropologist or social psychologist, depending on their inclinations. Bring a copy of your campus calendar to class and distribute it to your students, encouraging them to discuss the possibilities and decide which events will be most interesting to observe. Just about any event will provide a fruitful subject for this assignment's analysis, from a guest lecture to a concert to the spring dance. Remind students, too, that rituals can be as minor as raising a hand to be recognized or as stylized as singing the alma mater in a stadium. Depending on how involved you want students' papers to be, you might consider requiring them to study an event that occurs on a regular basis, whether weekly or annually. Major annual events offer the additional opportunity for students to research the activity's origins and changes over time.

Regardless of the scope of the event that students choose to analyze, require them to incorporate in their essays at least one of the findings Berreby cites; requiring two or three will give them more to work with and assure more thoughtful work. Their final papers should combine close observation, carefully recorded detail, and application of theory to the implications of an event they might otherwise have taken for granted.

Additional Resources

Nonfiction

Brad Land, *Goat: A Memoir* (2004)   After transferring to a new school, where his younger brother is already enrolled, Land decides to pledge a fraternity. In this memoir, he details the brutal hazing he endures.

Ayana D. Byrd and Lori L. Tharps, **The Rituals of Black Hair Culture** (p. 214)

Cultural attitudes and practices surrounding black hair have become the subject of scholarly inquiry relatively recently. With the late twentieth-century emergence of women's studies, African American studies, and American studies as independent academic disciplines, theorists have begun to seriously examine how mainstream white beauty standards affect gender and race relations. As Byrd and Tharps show, an identity marker as seemingly innocuous as hair can originate from long-standing cultural conflicts and the personal tensions that arise as a result.

Synthesizing some of the most influential theories of black hair politics, Byrd and Tharps suggest that black hair culture is a microcosm of the troubled history of black/white racial relations in America. As they explain it, "the many aspects of human adaptation—including language, technology, traditions, values, and social organization—are all identifiable components of the culture of Black hair in America" (par. 2). This summary may offer the best way to approach Byrd and Tharps's cultural analysis with your students. As a class, examine each of these aspects of culture as the authors present them in their essay. African American efforts to adapt to mainstream white beauty standards, as well as the concepts of "good" and "bad" black hair, for example, suggest an insidious internalization of white racism. Byrd and Tharps argue that the time-consuming technologies used to style black hair—from hot combs to chemical relaxers—are strongly tied to family rituals that can simultaneously create a bond among African Americans and reinforce their exclusion from mainstream white beauty culture. The black community exerts strong pressure on its members to conform to white ideals of beauty, even though taming "unruly" hair frequently involves physical pain.

It will be worthwhile, as well, to have your students examine how Byrd and Tharps structure their argument. They categorize black hair experiences into ritualized rites of passage that fuel the transition from childhood to adulthood and make it easier for African Americans to circulate in a white-majority culture but which also highlight that they are not a part of it. Note, too, that the authors relate conflicting opinions of several people whose experiences with black hair culture range from pride to trauma. Students may notice that the one constant in these anecdotes is a sense of difference—whether bad or good. You might ask them, then, how traditions of beauty and rites of passage affect community and individual identities.

For an additional narrative that relates an alternative approach to styling black hair, see Kathy Wilson's essay "Dude Looks Like a Lady" in chapter 1 (p. 21).

Interrogating Assumptions

As Byrd and Tharps present them, mainstream traditions marginalize black women and men by expecting them to adhere to a standard of beauty that is not readily supported by the natural characteristics of African American hair. The counter-traditions developed by the black community attempt both to approximate white-centered standards and to embrace difference. Byrd and Tharps suggest that although hair rituals promote unity among black people, they also perpetuate cultural and racial segregation.

Writing about Cultural Practices

This assignment calls for a position paper in which students must articulate and explain a position on a contested topic. To do this well, they will need to examine Byrd and Tharps's cultural analysis, looking for and questioning the authors' claims and the evidence they use to support them. At the same time, students will need to critically read an element of popular culture in order to support their own arguments. To keep them focused, you might suggest that they limit their analysis to a single, narrowly defined genre of popular culture expression, such as fashion magazines, daytime television advertising, or teen movies. You might suggest that they concentrate on a single example, such as a recent issue of *Cosmopolitan,* the commercials aired during one episode of *Passions,* or the movie *Clueless.*

Additional Resources

Fiction

bell hooks, *Happy to Be Nappy* (2001)   This children's book by the renowned social critic celebrates hair of all types.

Nonfiction

A'Lelia Bundles, *On Her Own Ground: The Life and Times of Madam C. J. Walker* (2001) An inventor and entrepreneur, Madam C. J. Walker made a considerable fortune from hair-care products marketed to African Americans.

Midge Wilson and Kathy Russell, *Divided Sisters: Bridging the Gap between Black Women and White Women* (1995) Wilson and Russell call for better understanding between black and white women. One aspect of their argument is the need for more-inclusive ideas of beauty.

Web

Nappturality, http://www.nappturality.com/ The bulletin boards and galleries on this site encourage African American women to embrace natural hair.

Garrison Keillor, **A Wobegon Holiday Dinner** (p. 225)

Keillor's memorable Thanksgiving narrative reveals that traditions are not always the result of consciously planned rituals. The interactions he describes have evolved over several family gatherings to the point that they're as predictable as the date of the event. And although they're not especially pleasant, they nonetheless serve to bond the family over common experiences. These rituals are a reference point that helps individual members determine and fulfill their roles in the family structure. Theoretically, the Thanksgiving holiday is a chance for Americans to connect with their colonial past and to celebrate a (mythic) historic moment of cooperation between the Pilgrims and Native Americans, but we see none of that in Keillor's story. For the Keillors, and for many families like them, Thanksgiving is primarily about celebrating family, not history.

What makes Mary Ann's vomiting episode especially significant is that it broke with family tradition. After a long day in which every aunt, uncle, parent, child, in-law, and cousin dutifully acted his or her part in the family ritual—from cooking to fighting to inexplicably weeping over the blessing—she surprised herself and everyone around her. Notice, though, how quickly and with determination the family reasserted normalcy. Perhaps subconsciously knowing that this would turn out to be the last of their "traditional" Thanksgiving meals, they shrugged off the anomaly and resumed the family ritual as though nothing out of the ordinary had taken place.

Students may notice that Keillor's yearnings to spend Thanksgiving with a different family also reveal that even the most established national traditions play out differently depending on the context and the participants. The rituals and meanings of Thanksgiving for Keillor's family are not the rituals and meanings shared by his fiancée's family, for example, or by "the Italians" as Keillor imagines them, or for Keillor and his new Danish wife and stepchildren 20 years later. Indeed, international students in your class may have no cultural context for understanding the American Thanksgiving as Keillor describes it, although the family tensions it invokes may ring true. If this is the case with your students, you might want to focus the discussion on annualized family gatherings in general, rather than Thanksgiving itself.

If you're interested in exploding myths about the origins of contemporary traditions, however, consider having your students research the history of the contemporary Thanksgiving celebration. They will quickly discover that the traditional menu of turkey, mashed potatoes, cranberries, and pumpkin pie was probably not the fare at the original 1621 harvest feast. They will surely be surprised to learn that our modern Thanksgiving holiday emerged in the mid-nineteenth century out of efforts to instill "American" values and behaviors in Eastern and Southern European immigrants and that the story of the "First Thanksgiving" shared by Pilgrims and Wampanoag Indians gained circulation only after the brutal Indian Wars of the late nineteenth century.

Writing about Cultural Practices

To help students get a feel for the critique of art this assignment calls for, spend some time in class analyzing Norman Rockwell's idealized image of the American family. A brief discussion of the history of *Freedom from Want* will open students' eyes. Although the painting has become the iconic image of Thanksgiving, most young people are unaware that Rockwell created it as part of a four-picture series of war propaganda. "The Four Freedoms" present a visual argument for American involvement in World War II. The freedoms Rockwell portrays—freedom of speech, freedom of worship, freedom from want, and freedom from fear—had been invoked by Franklin Delano Roosevelt in his January 6, 1941, State of the Union Address, in which he sought to convince both Congress and the American public that the United States should enter the war raging in Europe. This seemingly innocuous image of a family gathering for a meal was a warning that the cornerstones of American life—consumerism, family, and paternalism among them—were at imminent risk of being lost.

Additional Resources

Nonfiction

Catherine O'Neill Grace and Margaret M. Bruchac, *1621: A New Look at Thanksgiving* (2001)   Though the text is intended for younger readers, your students may find the photographs, from a more historically accurate Plimouth Plantation reenactment of the Thanksgiving story, interesting.

Web

Prairie Home Companion, http://prairiehome.publicradio.org/   Visitors can listen to past *Prairie Home Companion* radio shows on their website.

Film

Home for the Holidays (1995)   Holly Hunter plays the lead in this movie about the family tensions brought out by Thanksgiving.

Pieces of April (2003)   A young woman tries to reunite her estranged family by inviting them to Thanksgiving dinner at her apartment.

Natalie Guice Adams and Pamela J. Bettis, **Cheerleader! An American Icon** (p. 233)

In another part of the chapter from which this excerpt was taken, Adams and Bettis outline the history of American cheerleading. As they explain, the practice of shouting cheers originated in wartime battle cries and was adopted in 1869 by male spectators at a Princeton-Rutgers football game. By the early twentieth century, as organized college sports gained ground, administrators started establishing organized, all-male cheering squads to help fill "the need for institutional identity and proving one's loyalty to one's schools." The practice was not overwhelmingly approved of at first; indeed, critics complained of the overt and unrestrained expressions of emotion manifested by its participants. It wasn't until the late 1940s that cheerleading became a predominately female activity.

Cheerleading is again undergoing a transformation, moving from synchronized chants repeated by spectators toward elaborately choreographed dance routines. Understanding how drastically cheerleading has changed in the 150 or so years of its existence will help students recognize that this tradition is neither static (assumption 1) nor an authentic link to past American practices (assumption 2). The nature of the activity has changed as the American culture has changed. Yet somehow, the associations of cheerleading with optimism and support hold strong. Its methods may have changed, but cheerleading's original purposes—establishing group identification and bolstering group loyalty—have not.

Be sure to spend some time with your students exploring the wider implications of the authors' analysis of cheerleading as an American institution. If they at first see nothing wrong with applying cheerleading techniques to social and political causes, encourage your students to consider the connotations of the word "cheerleading" and how commentators tend to use the word when applying it to public figures. As Adams and Bettis suggest, in these contexts "cheerleading" implies a lack of critical attention to an issue. When the stakes are high, blind optimism can distract participants and observers from serious problems and potential solutions. At the same time, the infectious nature of cheering can exert pressure on dissenters to keep their objections to themselves.

Because perceptions of cheerleading tend to be either strongly positive or strongly negative, consider setting up a formal debate on the topic of whether cheerleading represents the best or the worst of American traits. Allow students to choose sides, or assign them to opposing teams. Each team should identify the points it will make and conduct additional research (beyond Adams and Bettis's essay) to support them. Be careful, however, not to let the debate degenerate into personal attacks on cheerleaders themselves. For the best results, the formalized discussion should focus on cheerleading as an institution and as a symbol of American identity.

For another exploration of optimism as a typically American trait, see David Brooks's "Our Sprawling, Supersize Utopia" (p. 139). For a discussion of how group identification fosters antagonism, see David Berreby's "It Takes a Tribe" (p. 207).

Interrogating Assumptions

As the authors suggest, cheerleading's quest for unity inevitably creates an "us-versus-them" dynamic. The cheers, after all, are designed to encourage competition. Although individual cheerleading squads may strive to build a sense of community among fans of their own teams, and although they may be friendly and welcoming toward competing teams and squads (par. 5), antagonism is an inherent aspect of their role. The same holds true when cheerleading techniques are used to support businesses and governments. The very act of building loyalty and support for a specific group tends to imagine an opposing group of "others" and a zero-sum game in which there must be a winner and a loser.

Writing about Cultural Practices

It may not be immediately apparent to your students that the key to this assignment lies in identifying the communication techniques associated with cheerleading. Explain to students that cheering goes beyond public performance. Marketing and public relations professionals often apply cheerleading methodologies to get their messages across. To help your students grasp this idea, you might consider gathering a few examples of "cheerleading" documents and bringing them to class. Work with your students to identify how messages of optimism, group identification, and loyalty are constructed to accomplish a specific purpose. Consider both what they include and what they leave out, and then send your students out to collect and analyze examples of their own. The final papers should include analysis of found documents as well as contemplation of the students' own cheerleading efforts.

Additional Resources

Film

Bring It On (2000)   While it follows standard teen-movie plotlines, this comedy also has some smartly drawn characters. As the head cheerleader of a suburban high school, Kirsten Dunst realizes that her predecessor stole routines from a largely African American inner-city school.

But I'm a Cheerleader! (1999)   To her surprise and confusion, a cheerleader is sent by her parents to a rehab camp for homosexuals. Using her cheering skills, she finds support among previously unlikely friends.

Video

"Smells Like Teen Spirit" (1991)   The video for Nirvana's first single exploits the imagery of cheerleading to suit their nonconformist stance. Their cheerleaders wear an anarchy symbol on their shirts.

Brent Staples, **The Star-Spangled Hard Hat** (p. 243)

In this intriguing cultural analysis of the hard hat Vice President Dick Cheney wore during a visit to Ground Zero following the attacks of September 11, Brent Staples offers an unconventional interpretation of the meanings—past and present—of the American flag. Underpinning his analysis is an implied argument about the meanings of "patriotism," which have been contested from the very beginnings of American history. Before you begin discussion of Staples's essay, therefore, you may want to explore with your class what patriotism means to them. Although many students may associate patriotism with unquestioning loyalty to the nation and its government, others might venture that a person can object to prevailing attitudes and U.S. policies while remaining patriotic. This idea is central to Staples's point about the new inclusiveness of the American flag.

In the days and weeks after the September 11, 2001, attacks, American flags became ubiquitous as a symbol of unity, of coming together despite cultural and political differences in a time of national and personal crisis. But as Staples reminds his readers, that same symbol was used during another war to establish disunity, fostering hostility and even violence between groups holding opposing perspectives of patriotism. Despite beliefs that tradition promotes unity (see assumption 3 in the chapter introduction), his examples from American history demonstrate that tradition can also be a powerful tool for silencing dissension and denying alternative perspectives.

Evolving attitudes toward nontraditional flags underscore another of the cultural dynamics examined in the chapter's introduction (assumption 1).

Postmodern and post–September 11 iterations of the American flag offer an excellent example of counter-traditions being co-opted by mainstream society. As Staples explains it, the Vietnam-era counterculture manipulated traditional images of the flag for its own uses, partly out of protest and partly as an effort to assert an American identity distinct from military policy. Decades later, those emblems of protest were being used as a symbol of patriotism by no less than the vice president of the United States. Whether this phenomenon illustrates hypocrisy or progress is open to debate.

Interrogating Assumptions

Staples vividly describes a specific instance in which a symbol of unity, the traditional American flag, occasioned disunity among the people who were expected to connect with something bigger than themselves—the United States of America. In some ways, disagreements over the proper uses of the flag were symptomatic of a larger rift between loyalists and antiwar protestors. During the 1960s and '70s, many Americans were vehemently opposed to the military actions being taken by their government and felt deeply alienated from it. Manipulating traditional images of the flag was a symbolic way to assert their American identity while rejecting American politics. Not surprisingly, many other Americans objected to what they considered a desecration of a sacred symbol and insisted that using it as a form of protest was tantamount to treason.

You may want to remind your students that although the American flag reemerged in September 2001 as a display of unity, the patriotism being expressed was a direct response to a foreign attack. This expression of unity among groups who were formerly in opposition was a direct expression of "us-versus-them" sentiment—Americans versus al Qaeda. Flag usage has subsided in the intervening years, but American cultural hostility toward Arab nations and peoples has intensified. Although the meaning of the flag may have evolved to include more Americans of more varied political stripes, it has also evolved as an expression of a new opposition.

Writing about Cultural Practices

This assignment asks students to work as semioticians. That is, it requires them to explore and articulate the implicit cultural meanings that infuse an everyday object or practice. To help ground their analyses, you might refer them to sections of Jack Solomon's *The Signs of Our Time: The Secret Meanings of Everyday Life*, which will give them a practical foundation in the practice of semiotic analysis, or simply inform them that analyzing the meanings of everyday things is an academic discipline unto itself.

Alternatively, you might suggest that students follow Brent Staples's lead and base their analyses in their personal experiences, either as willing participants/users of a cultural artifact or as dissenters. To add depth to their analyses, consider requiring them to conduct a little research on the history of the event or object they are studying. Keep in mind that many students will have connections to friends or relatives who either died on September 11 or who have served (and may still be serving) in Afghanistan or Iraq; the starting point for this essay assignment is potentially volatile as a result. Caution them not to let their analysis devolve into an opinion essay: Rather than preach on the benefits or dangers of patriotism, they should be careful to focus their essays on the cultural meanings of a patriotic symbol.

Additional Resources

Music

Bruce Springsteen, "Born in the U.S.A." (1984)   Ronald Reagan tried to use Springsteen's song in his 1984 campaign, overlooking its criticism of the Vietnam War. The cover of the *Born in the U.S.A.* album also features an iconic photograph by Annie Leibovitz of a rear view of Springsteen against a backdrop of the American flag.

Web

Aftershocks: 12 Months in NYC, http://www.newyorkmetro.com/news/ articles/wtc/1year/aftershocks/6.htm   An image of Dick Cheney wearing the hard hat Staples describes appears on the New York Metro website.

"Capture the Flag," http://slate.msn.com/?id=2905   Written at the time of a Jasper Johns retrospective, this Louis Menand article analyzes the artist's use of flag imagery.

Old Glory: The American Flag in Contemporary Art, http://artscenecal.com/ ArticlesFile/PhoenixMsmFile/PAMOldGlory.html   The Phoenix Art Museum presents a selection of works from an exhibit of flag images.

Jenn Shreve, A Fitting Memorial: The Commemorative T-Shirt (p. 248)

Although Shreve questions the appropriateness of memorial T-shirts, her musings on the subject reveal an important but often overlooked aspect of traditions. The growing popularity of new kinds of memorials suggests that traditions can lose their cultural power and that they don't endure forever. Eventually, even the strongest traditions may become stale and will be supplanted by something fresh that attempts to fulfill similar cultural functions.

In the case of grieving rituals and public memory, traditional memorials are gradually losing their relevance. The large-scale, permanent, publicly funded monuments that Shreve implies are the standard-bearer for public mourning are almost always reserved for cultural heroes or other important public figures.

They're expensive to create, and their placement must be negotiated among funding providers, government representatives, and public opinion. In general, they celebrate a record of accomplishment or mourn large-scale public tragedies. This kind of commemoration is out of reach for everyday people. They are especially unlikely to be provided for the gang members and victims of inner-city violence who, as Shreve explains, initiated the trend of memorial T-shirts. Although the public may not mourn these individuals, the people they leave behind must work through their grief all the same, and frequently they feel an obligation to assert the value of a life that was most likely not acknowledged by the mainstream public. T-shirts offer an ideal vehicle for fulfilling this need. Intensely personal, they are nonetheless difficult to ignore. Worn in public for everyday activities, the clothing thrusts personal tragedy into strangers' awareness, forcing others to recognize the value of a life lost to violence while it simultaneously "create[s] a sense of solidarity among wearers" (par. 6). Body art serves a similar purpose; encourage students to apply Shreve's points to a consideration of the September 11 tattoos pictured in chapter 1 (see p. 49).

Interrogating Assumptions

If students cling to the notion that visiting cemeteries is the proper venue for personal mourning, sharing the cultural history of modern burial grounds will reinforce the point that traditions are neither static nor permanent. Cemeteries did not emerge as sites for public mourning amid monuments until the mid-nineteenth century; the concept of the grave as a permanent resting place was invented in the 1840s as a commercial enterprise. When they first gained popularity, the cemeteries we associate with traditional mourning rituals were intended to serve double duty as recreational destinations (the modern urban cemetery predates the public park). A century and a half later, cemeteries no longer attract picnickers and casual strollers; their use is essentially limited to family members and close friends of the deceased, who typically visit only once or twice a year, if at all. Considering that some inner-city mourners may be unable to afford memorial markers or physically get to distant memorial parks, the commemorative power of cemeteries and public monuments has been diluted, and new ways of memorializing the dead have emerged to take their place. As the general public becomes less immune to the possibility of violent death in the wake of September 11, it makes sense that the counter-traditions invented by the disenfranchised have been adopted by the mainstream.

Writing about Cultural Practices

Consider structuring at least part of this assignment as a group project. Have members of your class suggest people or events that would not normally be eligible for a traditional monument, and encourage them to choose one of these subjects for their project. Instruct individual students to research the person or event they'll memorialize as well as the common elements of traditional memorials and share their findings with the class. They could consult published resources or conduct field work, depending on their proclivities. You may also want to explore the different kinds of nontraditional memorials that have gained popularity in recent years: Students may be aware of several of these forms, including inner-city wall murals, roadside shrines, memorial websites, petitions, musical performances, art exhibits, poetry collections, tattoos, jewelry, and quilts, among others. Using these alternatives as a starting point, the class can then work together to decide on the form of their nontraditional memorial and determine what shape it will take; they might then parcel out specific tasks to individual students. The memorial itself might be a group art project, or, if you think your students will be comfortable with the task, you might require each student to apply the class's findings to an individually created memorial. The critical analyses should be individually prepared papers.

Finally, depending on the quality and sensitivity of what your class produces, you may want to share the results with your community, either as a public exhibit or as a gift to the family of a deceased person.

Additional Resources

Scholarly Works

Jessica Mitford, *The American Way of Death Revisited* (1998) This revised edition of Mitford's 1963 classic looks into the funeral industry and explores how the workings of the business reveal our attitudes about death.

Web

Martha Cooper, NYC/Seen #1: Memorial Walls, http://photoarts.com/ cooper/index1.html   *PhotoArts Journal* published these images from Martha Cooper's series on memorial murals.

"Her Mission Is to Carry On for Those Who Can't," http://www.chron.com/ cs/CDA/ssistory.mpl/space/columbia/2985023   This article from the *Houston Chronicle* points to another growing form of tribute: people running marathons or other races in memoriam.

Gamaliel Padilla, **Moshing Etiquette** (p. 253)

A practice invented by punk-rock concertgoers in the late 1970s, moshing is a relatively recent phenomenon that is spreading to other upbeat music genres, particularly rock. Your students may at first have difficulty grasping what mosh pits could possibly have to do with the topic of tradition. Although you should be able to generate some interesting discussion about how traditions emerge when countercultural practices are co-opted by more mainstream groups, the better pedagogic utility of Padilla's article lies in its treatment of etiquette.

As the textbook suggests, most students will associate etiquette with fussy formal behavior restricted to the elite classes. In daily practice, however, it is a set of cultural rules established to ensure the comfort of all participants in any social setting. Like any kind of tradition, etiquette evolves as cultural and social contexts change, which is why etiquette guides from previous decades and centuries can seem so amusingly foreign to us. You may want to share with your students a few choice passages from a historic etiquette guide on the subject of dance. (An example from the nineteenth century: "When dancing with a lady you have never seen before, you should not talk to her much.") As new forms of social interaction emerge, new traditions emerge with them to guide participants' behaviors and social interactions and to prevent injury, whether emotional or physical. It may be useful to review Padilla's paragraphs one by one and identify the ways in which her etiquette rules protect both moshing participants and observers. Although moshing originally developed as a punk-rock celebration of chaos and violence, as it becomes more mainstream, behavioral rules are emerging to tame it. You may want to ask your students where else they have seen this dynamic take place and how it affected them.

Writing about Cultural Practices

This project offers an inventive way to cap your class's study of traditions. There are plenty of emerging social settings for which students might propose rules, from hosting a Texas hold 'em party to using wireless Internet hot spots in public locations. If they have difficulty imagining any situations that call for new rules of etiquette, consider encouraging students to name possibilities out loud while you keep a running tally on the board. Alternatively, you might offer the option of updating the etiquette rules for a long-running social tradition that has seen recent changes, such as same-sex weddings or baby showers for international adoptions. Whatever topic they choose to tackle, students should take their new understanding of the origins and functions of traditions to establish a new cultural tradition of their own.

Additional Resources

Nonfiction

Judith Martin, *Miss Manners' Guide to Excruciatingly Correct Behavior, Freshly Updated* (2005)   The most prominent current voice on etiquette, Martin advocates politesse without stodginess.

Peggy Post, *Emily Post's Etiquette* (2004)   Starting with her first publication in 1922, Emily Post was a preeminent authority on social graces. Recent versions have been updated by her great-granddaughter-in-law.

Web

Etiquette Hell, http://www.etiquettehell.com   A different kind of etiquette manual, *Etiquette Hell* allows users to post examples of truly egregious behavior, most of it relating to weddings.

Mixing Words and Images:
Inventing a New Holiday (p. 257)

This project might best be accomplished in teams. By working together, students can brainstorm and build off each other's ideas to create a holiday that incorporates a rich multitude of elements and meanings. Team members will be able to help each other identify what the holiday must entail, and collaboration will help ensure that nothing is overlooked.

Inventing a holiday and designing a poster to promote it will likely be fun for your students. Keep in mind, however, that their purpose is to determine how values and beliefs are expressed through traditions. To this end, you may want to encourage them to draft their analyses *before* they design their posters. At the very least, students should make some attempt to answer the questions on page 257 before they start crafting the visual element of the project. Students' efforts will be more productive if they determine in advance who their audience is, what practices and values audience members already share, what the purpose of a new holiday might be, and what kinds of rituals might help to express and cement their target community's beliefs.

To help your students think creatively, you might explore as a class unusual holidays that already exist and what kinds of values they promote. Some possible examples include Talk Like a Pirate Day (see http://www.talklikeapirate.com), Bubble Wrap Appreciation Day, Reconciliation Day (an Ann Landers favorite), National Nothing Day, Middle Children's Day, and National Whiner's Day. For a comprehensive listing of American holidays—major and minor, serious and wacky—refer your students to *Chase's Calendar of Events* (McGraw-Hill), which is updated annually.

Connecting to Culture: Suggestions for Writing (p. 258)

The writing assignments that conclude the chapter offer students an opportunity to synthesize the ideas they've encountered in the readings and to make some conclusions about the assumptions outlined in the chapter introduction.

Rocking the Mainstream: An Analysis of Counter-Traditions

For this assignment, students will identify, research, and analyze a cultural practice that originated as a form of resistance to mainstream traditions. As the assignment points out, the possibilities for topics are nearly endless. Encourage your students to choose a counter-tradition that they are at least somewhat familiar with and that relates to an area of personal interest—such as alternative music, ethnic affiliations, a hobby, a political movement, or a subculture that they consider themselves to be a part of. Remind them that traditions now considered mainstream, such as Mother's Day, may have started as counter-traditions. Remind them, as well, that they don't need to stick to campus traditions if they don't want to, although localizing their investigation will simplify their research. If possible, students might interview the founders or some of the participants of the counter-tradition they will write about; they might also search for archival or published documents that express the group's purpose in starting their counter-tradition. Final papers should describe a counter-tradition, relate its history in some detail (with accurate documentation of sources), and analyze its function and meanings for participants.

Defining America: A Look at Civic Rituals and Public Spectacles

This cultural-analysis assignment asks students to observe a public event, describe it in detail, and analyze it as a cultural event. Objectivity will come more easily if students choose an event or a spectacle that they wouldn't normally participate in. You might encourage them to take photographs and incorporate them, as well as images from flyers, into their analyses as well. To help students support their interpretations of what they see, consider requiring a minimal amount of background research into the origins and history of the event that they will observe; they might also interview an organizer or some of the people in attendance.

For a book-length study of the political uses of public spectacles in early American history, see David Waldstreicher, *In the Midst of Perpetual Fetes: The Making of American Nationalism, 1776–1820* (1997).

Interrogating Assumptions: How Do Traditions Define Us?

The most formal of the writing projects in this chapter, this final assignment calls for a text-based comparative analysis that synthesizes ideas from the chapter and several individual readings. To ensure coherence, encourage students to select readings that are closely related thematically as well as in the manner in which they address assumptions about tradition. If you've assigned any of the Interrogating Assumptions or Connecting to Another Reading questions that follow some of the selections in the chapter, allow your students to use their responses as starting points for their drafts. A successful student essay will posit a thesis about one of the assumptions and use the readings to support it, rather than simply compare and contrast several selections.

4 Romance

. . . or, what's love got to do with it?

Love is not as natural as most of us tend to believe. History, science, and scholarship have shown that almost everything associated with romance, from sexual identity to dating rituals to the marriage contract, is shaped and reshaped by culture. Even something as seemingly immutable as the sexual experience changes over time: Enlightenment beliefs that a woman could not become pregnant without achieving orgasm gave way to the Victorian assumption that women received no pleasure from sex, which was widely accepted as truth until the mid-twentieth century, when Alfred Kinsey suggested otherwise. If cultural assumptions can influence physical reactions, nothing about romance is static. Indeed, things we take for granted today, such as companionate marriage and modern depictions of gay identity, would have been unimaginable for our great-great-grandparents. Likewise, aspects of their romantic reality, such as the legal position that adultery was a betrayal of the state, seem unimaginable today. Romance, in other words, is a cultural construction.

Although students who have experienced the joys and heartaches of romance might consider themselves experts on the subject, some may not have given much critical thought to how love is shaped by culture or where their own romantic inclinations come from. Before you have them read the chapter introduction, you may want to explore, as a class or through a preliminary journal assignment, what assumptions your students currently hold about their own experiences with and expectations of love. Brainstorm as a group what "romance" means and what contributes to it. What is the difference between love and romance? Without getting too personal, what do students expect from romantic partners (past, present, or future)? What have their partners expected of them? How have students' understanding of relationships changed over time? What is the ideal romantic relationship, and why do people strive for it?

Because the central assumptions outlined in the chapter's introduction form the basis for analyzing the chapter's readings, spend some time discussing them in class. Use the questions that follow each discussion of an assumption to explore the concept with your students. You might want to ask your students whether they agree or disagree with the outlined assumptions, and what other assumptions about romance they can identify. Discuss with your class, also, how these assumptions function in American culture: Who holds them? What purposes do they serve? Are they helpful or harmful? And how do students see them played out in their personal lives and in the world around them?

As the *Onion* story and Examining the Everyday assignment that open the chapter humorously suggest, American notions of romance are riddled with cliché, unrealistic expectations, miscommunication, and dangerous behavior. Even the most utilitarian items, like ladders, become infused with cultural meaning in the context of romance. Before students tackle the Examining the Everyday assignment, consider spending some time analyzing the symbolism of ladders in the context of the *Onion* story. Romantic portrayals of climbing to a beloved's window permeate the Western cultural tradition, from *Rapunzel* to *Romeo and Juliet* to *Pretty Woman*. But what makes a ladder romantic? Prod your students to consider both its physical appearance (two parallel lines connected to each other) and its cultural connotations (a ladder enables a person to reach new heights, but it also poses a danger of injury). With a little in-class practice analyzing symbolism, students will be better prepared to interpret the romantic imagery used for various purposes in American culture, for example, to sell a product.

Like the opening story, all of the readings in this chapter question one or several of the four main assumptions outlined in the introduction—love conquers all; "chemistry" equals love; true loves are soul mates; true love is forever. In an engaging personal account, David Sedaris takes issue with Hollywood portrayals of romance, using humor and his own experience to warn that such portrayals fuel unrealistic expectations and do harm to real relationships, while bell hooks describes her grandparents' unconventional marriage to call into question prevailing ideas about the ideal romantic partnership. Looking at how romance has changed in the last generation, Jennifer Egan examines the recent phenomenon of Internet dating to determine how technology may be affecting the way we pursue new love interests, and Caitlin Leffel examines published wedding announcements in a consideration of how marriage has been transformed by modernity. Ellen Fein and Sherrie Schneider, Samantha Daniels, and Dave Singleton offer cultural artifacts in the form of dating guides for students to analyze, while Sasha Cagen, in "People Like Us: The Quirkyalones," argues the benefits of being single by choice. Jon Katz offers a cultural analysis of how some people rely on their pets to fill companionship voids. Taking an academic approach to the idea that love and romance are socially constructed, Laura Kipnis presents an iconoclastic argument against the institution of marriage and Scott Russell Sanders examines how cultural influences have shaped how men look at women. And echoing Sanders's analysis of physical attraction, Benedict Carey summarizes recent scientific studies that map the connection between infatuation and brain chemistry.

The strong personal relevance of the topic combined with the relative ease of debunking the assumptions that surround romance make chapter 4 an excellent starting point for a cultural studies course that emphasizes analysis; it's also a natural opening for a composition course that follows a progression from personal to argumentative writing. Alternatively, if you're teaching in the spring term you might want to time your focus on this chapter to coincide with Valentine's Day.

Additional Resources

Nonfiction

John D'Emilio and Estelle B. Freedman, *Intimate Matters: A History of Sexuality in America* (1988)   A broad synthesis of scholarship on sexuality and cultural constructions of love, *Intimate Matters* complicates the idea that sexual attitudes have followed a constant trend toward greater freedom.

Leila J. Rupp, *A Desired Past: A Short History of Same-Sex Love in America* (1999)   Rupp looks to Native American and African, as well as European, attitudes to understand the history of homosexuality in America. She also looks beyond urban centers to find gay communities throughout the country.

Music

David Bowie, "Modern Love," and Yeah Yeah Yeahs, "Modern Romance" These two songs, from 1983 and 2003 respectively, both take a skeptical view of contemporary romance.

Film

50 First Dates (2004)   Adam Sandler plays a commitment phobe who finally falls in love only to discover that his girlfriend's short-term memory loss causes her to forget him every morning.

David Sedaris, **The End of the Affair** (p. 272)

David Sedaris and Hugh Hamrick met through mutual friends and have been a couple since 1990. Although Sedaris writes about their relationship frequently, he never idealizes it. In this essay from his recent book, he explores one of the major differences between himself and his partner: Hugh is a romantic, and David is not.

American romantic expectations are strongly influenced by Hollywood, but as Sedaris demonstrates, those expectations not only are unrealistic but also can cause strife within a real-life relationship. For him, love is not a matter of passion or drama—it's comprised of shared interests and mutual support, and it's inherently mundane. Because he has no patience for Hollywood portraits of romance, it flusters him that his partner can be so affected by melodrama while overlooking the stability of their long-term relationship. Sedaris clearly rejects the ideas of passionate attraction (assumption 2) and finding a soul mate (assumption 3), but your students may notice that he embraces other assumptions about love: that it overcomes adversity (assumption 1), for one, and that it lasts forever (assumption 4). Expecting that he and Hugh will misunderstand each other and fight from time to time, he doesn't worry that their differences will split them up. Indeed, Sedaris suggests that fights are the only way to spark passion after more than a decade together.

Some students may be troubled by Sedaris's apparent acceptance of violence in his relationship. You may want to explore this issue with them. Ask your students, first of all, whether they think Sedaris and Hamrick truly battle each other physically or if Sedaris invented the episode for humorous effect. What clues in the text lead them to their conclusions? And how does Sedaris's attempt at humor affect them? Is the fight funny, or does it suggest something darker about how idealized expectations of love influence personal relationships?

Interrogating Assumptions

As Sedaris describes them, Hollywood portrayals of romance are not simply unrealistic, they emphasize loss or failure. Too many love stories, for example, center on the premature death of one of the lovers, on the idea that true love never makes it past the courtship stage. Hollywood's reliance on the star-crossed-lovers plotline allows movies and television dramas to celebrate the passion and chemistry often experienced at the beginning of a relationship, but it also implies that love can be nothing but temporary. This is deeply troubling for Sedaris, who finds the comfort and stability in his "boring" long-term relationship far more satisfying than the conflict glamorized in movies.

Writing about Cultural Practices

This assignment calls for a cultural analysis of how romance is depicted in a single film. You may want to screen a movie and require that the entire class write about it, or you might opt to give them more choices (see below for some film suggestions). Either way, it will be useful to explain to your students that conflict is central to an effective plot; without it, there is rarely much of a story to tell. Discourage your students from simply identifying how a Hollywood portrayal of romance is unrealistic. Stress, instead, that they are to examine the plot of a movie with the traditional romance formula, noting where it sticks to convention and where it departs from it and assessing how the filmmaker manipulates cultural assumptions about romance. For this to work, you will almost certainly need to work with the class to outline the conventions of Hollywood romance.

In addition to the films mentioned in the chapter's introduction, promising romantic comedies for the assignment include:

How Stella Got Her Groove Back	*Something's Gotta Give*
Never Been Kissed	*Ten Things I Hate about You*
Sideways	*When Harry Met Sally . . .*

In addition to *The End of the Affair*, promising dramas include:

Casablanca	*Love Story*
The English Patient	*Sid & Nancy*
House of Flying Daggers	*Wuthering Heights*

Additional Resources

Fiction

Graham Greene, *The End of the Affair* (1951)   The basis of the movie Sedaris writes about, *The End of the Affair* concerns the liaison of a novelist and a married woman during World War II. They survive the bombing of London, but their relationship changes drastically.

Film

The Quiet American (2002)   Based on another Graham Greene novel, this film stars Michael Caine as Thomas Fowler, a jaded British reporter in Vietnam. Brendan Fraser, as a rigidly upright American, gets involved in a love triangle when he tries to win over Fowler's beautiful Vietnamese mistress.

Web

Photos: People in Love, http://www.pcimagenetwork.com/love/love.html
These stock photos, which betray some of our clichés about how love looks, may provide a comparison with students' image of Sedaris and his partner.

Jennifer Egan, **Love in the Time of No Time** (p. 275)

Egan's exploration of the online dating world opens with the assertion that it has radically transformed romantic relationships but closes with the premise that the Internet has simply helped people overcome the chaos of modern living. You may want to begin classroom discussion, therefore, by asking your students to identify and contemplate Egan's overarching thesis. What question does she pose, and what does she conclude? The answers aren't immediately apparent.

Either as a take-home assignment or an in-class exercise, ask your students to catalog the ways in which, according to Egan, the Internet has changed modern dating practices. You might also want to brainstorm a comparative list of the practices, expectations, and norms generally associated with "traditional" dating and online dating. (It would be helpful to assign Egan's essay in conjunction with the dating rules proposed by Ellen Fein and Sherrie Schneider, Samantha Daniels, and Dave Singleton on pages 296–306.) Despite Egan's emphasis on how the Internet may be altering modern relationships, many older people who use dating websites would insist that dating hasn't changed all that much. Web services vastly increase the pool of potential dates, but the actual practice of dating—with its heady anticipations, false starts, giddy first meetings, frustrations, rude behaviors, miscommunications, and occasional successes—is the same perplexing experience it's always been. Indeed, the people most disappointed by online romance are often the people who expect the efficiencies of the Internet to eliminate the hassles and heartaches of searching for a mate. After comparing online and real-world dating and after considering Egan's evidence, ask your students whether her argument rings true. Has the Internet really changed the crux of how people approach romance, or has it merely provided new conduits for behaviors that have remained constant? Press your students to offer evidence for whatever conclusions they reach.

For instructors committed to *ReMix*'s "assumptions" pedagogy, examining Egan's extended discussion of chemistry will prove especially fruitful. In theory, online dating subordinates the role of attraction in dating, giving initial priority to the aspects of a relationship that chemistry often overshadows: shared interests, values, and goals. Searching objective data in profiles allows the romantically inclined to weed out patently bad matches before initiating contact, reducing the chances of disappointment, struggle, and wasted time while increasing the chances of finding a perfect mate. But as most online daters quickly discover, chemistry and affinity are unpredictable. Egan worries that online daters overemphasize the quest for that initial spark, often dismissing a potential mate before an emotional bond has had a chance to form. How, you might ask your students, does her concern complicate the assumption that chemistry equals love? The assumption that soul mates love each other for who they are, regardless of physical attraction?

Writing about Cultural Practices

Both of the assignments that follow "Love in the Time of No Time" ask students to take up Marshall McLuhan's famous idea that the medium is the message. The first assignment emphasizes how a particular medium (the online dating profile) imposes meaning on the messages a person sends; the second assignment emphasizes how different media (email, instant messaging, and telephone calls) influence the way a message is interpreted. In each case, students will need to examine the structures and limitations imposed by communication technology and to assess how a particular medium affects the content of interpersonal communications. Note that the second assignment will be more productive if you teach Egan's essay in conjunction with the cluster of dating rules on pages 296–306.

Nonfiction

Marshall McLuhan, *Understanding Media: The Extensions of Man* (1964)
McLuhan's landmark book explores the effects of media on the way people
live. Some of the terminology he uses in talking about the media revolution
has become integral to our daily speech.

Television

Single in the City   This show, produced by the WE network, is heavily influenced by *Sex and the City.* In this reality version, viewers follow the dating
lives of New York career women.

Radio

Fresh Air, http://www.npr.org/templates/rundowns/ rundown.php?prgId
=13&prgDate=17-Aug-05   In this episode of *Fresh Air,* Terry Gross interviews the founder of E-Harmony, a website that attempts to match people
not on what they say they want but on what a questionnaire reveals about
their personalities. Gross also interviews the originators of Speed Dating,
which began as a way for Jewish singles in Los Angeles to meet.

Sasha Cagen, **People Like Us: The Quirkyalones** (p. 292)

Students may at first have some trouble resolving the apparent contradictions of
Cagen's position: How can a person who chooses to be alone be a romantic?
Especially for young adults who may put a strong value on coupling, the concept
may be foreign. Part of the answer lies in the subtitle of Cagen's book: Her use
of the adjective "uncompromising" suggests that quirkyalones simply refuse to
lower their romantic standards. But what exactly are those standards, and where
did they come from? Exploring Cagen's essay in the context of the chapter introduction's assumptions—particularly the idea that every one of us has a soul mate
somewhere—will help students develop a more complex understanding of her
argument.

Cagen's manifesto illustrates a central paradox of contemporary romance:
Idealism prolongs singlehood. Culturally fueled expectations of finding never
ending passion with a soul mate cause many to view dating as a waste of time.
Some choose to be alone as they patiently wait for their perfect partner to mate-
rialize. As Cagen describes it, this is a healthy and productive attitude that keeps
quirkyalones from wallowing in loneliness. But is it? You might want to ask your
students whether they read any defensiveness in Cagen's argument. Where does
she hint that being alone isn't as liberating as she claims it is? Has she truly freed

herself from cultural pressures to find a partner, or does the very act of resisting those expectations suggest that they still have a hold on the writer? Furthermore, what does it suggest about contemporary culture that people like Cagen are compelled to defend their single status?

Interrogating Assumptions

Students should recognize that Cagen and other quirkyalones would most strongly identify with the assumption that a person's true love will be a soul mate. Several comments in the essay reinforce the idea that "that perfect someone" is out there somewhere. Cagen explains, for example, that "out of millions, we have to find the one who will understand" (par. 5) and that "when we do find a match, we verge on obsessive" (8). To some extent, quirkyalones are also looking for passion and chemistry, "living for the exhilaration of meeting someone new" and the possibility of "momentous meetings" (6). Notice, however, that Cagen suggests that the possibility of finding a soul mate is also frightening. The longer a quirkyalone waits for the perfect match, the more fixed he or she becomes in a "social constellation" of multiple "significant others" (11).

Writing about Cultural Practices

In some ways, this assignment puts students in the position of being the subjects of a sociological experiment. Encourage students not only to examine how others at the event interact with them and with each other but also to pay close attention to their own feelings. Extroverted students may have no trouble with the idea of attending an event alone, but introverted or shy students might well be terrified at the prospect. If this is the case with anyone in your class, allow them the option of limiting their time at the event (to 10 or 15 minutes, maybe) and encourage them to analyze their trepidation as part of their papers: Why can attending a social event alone be an intimidating prospect? Students' final papers should combine a detailed description of the event and its participants' interactions, and it should include a considered analysis of how social pressures to form romantic partnerships influence people's social behavior.

Additional Resources

Nonfiction

Rainer Maria Rilke, *Letters to a Young Poet* (1934)   A prototype of the quirkyalone, Rilke paints for a young aspirant a romantic picture of artistic solitude.

Film

Breakfast at Tiffany's (1961)   Audrey Hepburn is the self-christened Holly Golightly, a young woman who moves to New York to pursue her romantic fantasies.

Web

Quirkyalone, http://www.quirkyalone.net   Cagen's website includes a quiz to determine whether or not one is a quirkyalone as well as a list of "Quirky" award–winning musicians, movies, and so on.

"Glad to Be Asexual," http://www.newscientist.com/article.ns?id=dn6533   This article from *New Scientist* magazine observes a new phenomenon of people who aren't interested in sex.

CLUSTERED READINGS: FOCUS ON DATING RULES

Ellen Fein and Sherrie Schneider, **Don't Talk to a Man First** (p. 296)

Samantha Daniels, **20 Simple Tips for the Perfect Date** (p. 299)

Dave Singleton, *From* **The MANdates: 25 Real Rules for Successful Gay Dating** (p. 300)

These excerpts are best approached as cultural artifacts, or documents that reveal the hidden realities of their time and place. Generally, advice is offered in the guise of solving a problem. Encourage your students, then, to look past the nuggets of advice in an effort to identify the problems that these authors are tackling on their readers' behalf, keeping in mind the different intended audience for each reading. You might want to keep a running list of the social and cultural challenges implied by the advice offered in each reading. Ask your students the following questions: What issues do these writers' audiences have in common? What problems seem to be unique to straight women? Straight men? Gay men? What romantic problems do these groups share?

The writers' desire to offer advice reveals a shared cultural belief that there's something unnatural or at least complicated about romance. As these writers describe things, relationships require both partners to make a conscious effort to override their instincts or at least their habits. Implicitly, they agree with Scott Russell Sanders (see "Looking at Women," p. 329) and Laura Kipnis (see "Against Love," p. 308), who argue that romantic love is a social construction. Attraction may be biologically driven, but relationships and emotions are largely determined by cultural norms that we absorb unconsciously and come to accept as natural. Dating is difficult at least partly because successful relationships require an understanding of prevailing cultural expectations as well as a fluency in learned behaviors that often go against what may feel right. These advice manuals attempt both to unveil those expectations and to teach the appropriate behaviors that go with them.

Interrogating Assumptions

Each excerpt reveals different assumptions about the nature of romance. Ellen Fein and Sherrie Schneider, for instance, reject the idea that love is a romantic partnership between soul mates, asserting, instead, that relationships are part of a never-ending battle of the sexes in which men and women struggle for power over each other. It is a corollary of the assumption that love is always beset by obstacles. For women to win this battle, the authors insist that they must subvert their desires and assume a counterintuitive passivity designed to manipulate men into filling their emotional needs.

Although Dave Singleton makes a point of refuting several of the more galling assumptions that ground the *Rules,* Samantha Daniels shares Fein and Schneider's belief that men should be active and women passive. All three readings build on the assumption that relationships will be presented with obstacles, but none assumes that love can overcome problems. Instead, the problem is finding true love (or a close approximation of it) in the first place.

All three sets of advice assume, as well, that dating is a goal-oriented activity. For Fein and Schneider, the goal is marriage and the comfortable stability that is supposed to go with it. For Daniels, the goal is sex. Singleton argues that several goals are possible but determines that the minimum goal for a dating couple should be avoidance of conflict. You might ask your students why none of these writers considers the possibility of dating for its own sake.

Writing about Cultural Practices

If students balk at the idea of reading a complete book for one assignment, point out that most contemporary dating guides can be read in one sitting lasting a couple of hours. You might offer the option of focusing on a book's introduction or a single chapter, but reading the advice straight through will give students a much better understanding of the authors' approach. If books are hard to locate, note that most online dating sites include voluminous tips for success; these sources would also work well.

If you'd rather keep the focus on printed books, encourage your students to search for advice from at least two or three generations back. Older how-to guides will be easier and more productive for students to examine. Being removed from the culture that produced the advice, students will be better equipped to read them with an analytic eye. Also promising would be for students to examine advice aimed at a demographic group of which they are not a part. Male students might read advice for women, heterosexual students might read advice for lesbians, white students might read advice aimed at Chicanas, and so on.

Additional Resources

Fiction

Melissa Bank, *The Girl's Guide to Hunting and Fishing* (1999)   Having been failed by the manual *How to Meet and Marry Mr. Right,* Bank's heroine has to negotiate a world of relationships without quite understanding its rules.

Film

Bridget Jones's Diary (2001)   A thirtysomething "singleton" sets herself, with mixed success, rules for improving her love life.

Kissing Jessica Stein (2001)   Adapted from the play *Lipschtick,* a young professional woman, having grown frustrated with her own self-imposed rules for dating, decides to broaden her horizons.

Television

Who Wants to Marry My Dad?   Traditional roles are reversed in this reality show as adult children give their father advice on potential mates.

Laura Kipnis, **Against Love** (p. 308)

Kipnis has stressed that "Against Love" (both the article and the book) is a polemic, acknowledging that her writing is deliberately provocative in an effort to stir up thoughtful debate. The title, however, is somewhat misleading. Kipnis is not arguing against love but rather against the institution of marriage—which she claims has become an agent of social control—and against cultural expectations that a monogamous romantic relationship can remain fulfilling for a lifetime—which she insists is simply impossible. Academic reviewers have applauded her nerve and her wit but faulted her methodology, arguing that Kipnis fails to cite sufficient sources, follow the rules of logic, or fully consider the implications of her proposal. Many general readers have been offended by what they consider Kipnis's cavalier dismissal of the value of marriage. Other readers, however, have seen themselves in her anecdotes, allowing them to consider with an open mind her arguments in favor of adultery.

Because Kipnis is so provocative, you may want to start discussion by gathering your students' initial reactions to her essay. Does it make them angry, confused, defensive, intrigued? And what is it about her stance that threatens so many readers? You might want to remind your class that marriage is a hot-button issue at the moment: As leaders of the gay rights movement push for the option of marriage and the personal and economic benefits that come with it, a large contingency of Americans have rallied to establish a legal definition of marriage as a lifetime commitment between one man and one woman. In the current cultural climate, which is rife with a heated exchange of ideas, Kipnis's defiant devaluation of marriage takes on serious political implications.

What may be most surprising to students is that Kipnis's argument is grounded in historical truth. For centuries, marriage had been an economic and political institution that assured traceable lineages, cemented political alliances (in the case of upper classes), and pooled labor and financial resources. Although romantic love may have bloomed in such formalized relationships, it wasn't necessarily expected to. American culture has long presumed that marriage is the cornerstone of social and political stability, to the point that many states' laws equated adultery with treason through the nineteenth century. The idea of marriage as a loving partnership between equals, which today we take for granted as natural, was a twentieth-century invention.

You might consider telling your students, however, that despite her emphasis on historical constructions of love and marriage, Kipnis ignores some equally significant historical truths. Divorce rates might well be higher than they've ever been, for example, simply because changes in state laws made divorce more accessible in the mid-twentieth century and because women have gained levels of economic independence unfathomable before the 1970s. Students may be surprised to learn, as well, that from the onset of the Victorian era until Alfred Kinsey's publication of *Sexual Behavior in the Human Female* (1953), women were presumed to have no sexual desires of their own.

The textbook's focus on assumptions will prove especially useful in analyzing "Against Love." Kipnis takes pains to reject the assumptions that love conquers all, that each person has one soul mate, and that love lasts forever. Students might notice, however, that Kipnis rests her argument on the idea that lust and sexual excitement are the true foundations of romantic happiness. Although the author fails to acknowledge or question this central assumption, encourage your students to explore the implications of her reliance on it.

Writing about Cultural Practices

This assignment asks students to analyze song lyrics as cultural artifacts that can reveal broad-based attitudes about romance. Encourage them to focus on two or three songs, but stress that because effective writing argues a point, their essays will be most successful if students choose songs that are thematically connected to each other. That thematic connection should help lead them to a critical analysis that they can support with evidence from the lyrics. The possibilities for thematic links are endless, but you might suggest that students consider songs penned by the same songwriter or performed by the same artist, selections from a movie soundtrack, popular wedding ballads, "cheating heart" lamentations, breakup songs, make-out music, or lyrics that dwell on sexuality, monogamy, promiscuity, and so on.

Additional Resources

Nonfiction

Michel Foucault, *The History of Sexuality: An Introduction* (1978)   Foucault attempts to understand why humans are driven to talk and think about sexuality so much and suggests that sexual identities are shaped by political and economic forces.

Hendrik Hartog, *Man and Wife in America: A History* (2000)   Looking into judicial records, Hartog constructs a history of marriage rooted in its legal aspects.

Poetry

Eavan Boland, *Against Love Poetry* (2001)   Boland rejects the glorification of love in traditional poems for a more realistic expression of marital love.

bell hooks, **Baba and Daddy Gus** (p. 318)

Bell hooks wrote this essay to explain how her grandparents' eccentricities inspired her to think, act, and write as she does, but she also offers some telling insights into the inner workings of a successful marriage. Profoundly different from one another and apparently not a passionate couple, Sarah and Gus Oldham, as hooks once said in an interview, were nonetheless happily married for 75 years. Hooks doesn't say so directly, but she suggests that the key to their relationship was a mutual respect for individuality and a disregard for popular ideals of romantic love.

Both "Baba" and "Daddy Gus" bucked cultural expectations regarding gender roles and romance. As hooks describes, family and community members scorned her grandfather for not being manly. He was calm, quiet, pacifistic, and tender, and (as others interpreted it) he allowed his wife to control him. "Baba," on the other hand, was strong, outspoken, aggressive, and distant—feminine only in her love of quilting. Objectively, theirs was not a conventional marriage. They slept in separate rooms, displayed no affection, pursued conflicting interests, had different ideas about child rearing, and held strongly opposing religious values; they barely seemed to like each other. But as hooks explains, they relied on each other in ways too deep to comprehend from a distance. The Oldhams may not have been soul mates as the idea prevails in the popular imagination—each had a full and independent life that partly excluded the other—but they understood and complemented each other in ways nobody else could. Their unconventional relationship allowed both partners to be fully themselves, without expectations of compromise or sacrifice.

Hooks once defined love as "a combination of six things: care, knowledge, responsibility, respect, trust, and commitment." You might ask your students how the Oldhams' relationship may have contributed to their iconoclastic grand-daughter's own ideas about love and marriage.

Interrogating Assumptions

The advantages of being in a marriage in which two people are as different from each other as hooks's grandparents are extend beyond the union itself. As a child, hooks is exposed to drastically different approaches to social interaction, religion, education, and what it means to stand up for oneself. Discourse in the marriage creates discourse in the family; in short, it encourages criticism and introspection.

The drawback is that, although hooks's grandparents clearly experienced a kind of intimacy beyond the family's understanding, tenderness and affection gave way to fighting—an easier kind of passion. Still, it remains that their marriage was a close one. A couple does not necessarily have to share opinions, a faith, or even a bed to maintain respect and caring in the marriage.

Writing about Cultural Practices

There is some risk that students will resort to simple plot summary and miss the point of this assignment, which is to examine how a culture's romantic assumptions are revealed in the stories it tells. To ensure critical engagement with the examples students choose, you might instruct them to begin their papers with a one-paragraph plot summary and devote the rest of their essays to analyzing the couple's relationship. Consider, too, that students will probably do better to focus on a single story rather than attempt to address multiple examples, unless the examples are very closely related (such as an original film and its sequel). Whatever they choose to study, remind them that they will need to do more than describe their examples. Successful papers will develop an argument not only about how difference fuels romantic attraction but also about how their fictional example uses romantic assumptions to tell its story.

Additional Resources

Nonfiction

bell hooks, *All About Love: New Visions* (2000)   By attempting to untangle sex and love, hooks addresses what she sees as the transformative spiritual possibilities of love.

———, *Salvation: Black People and Love* (2001)   Hooks returns to the subject of love to propose that it may be a powerful force for social change.

Poetry

Rita Dove, *Thomas and Beulah* (1986)   Dove's book, based to some extent on her own grandparents, sketches both the lives of two individuals and the complexities of their marriage.

Web

bell hooks, "Loving Rightly," http://www.mprsnd.org/interview/hooks.htm
This partial transcript of comments following a lecture hooks gave at
Washington University provides further elaboration of her ideas in
Salvation.

Jon Katz, **Petophilia** (p. 325)

Despite its humor, Jon Katz's essay unearths a common problem with romance:
Interpersonal relationships can be as much a source of pain and frustration as
of happiness. Whether stung by rejection or wounded by a bad relationship,
however, most of us feel a primal need to connect emotionally with another living being. If humans are disappointing, animals can fill the gap for many. But
as Katz explains, substituting animal companionship for human romance can be
unhealthy and just a little weird.

Students may at first resist this reading, insisting that it's silly and off topic.
The silliness of "Petophilia," however, is its strength. Katz's classification of dog
love (see pars. 11–13) meshes nicely with the assumptions outlined in the chapter's introduction. Explain to your students what anthropomorphism is, then ask
them to replace the animals in Katz's examples with humans. These pet owners'
exaggerated ideas of their animals' feelings underscore the flaws of one of the
major assumptions about love: that a person's true love will be a soul mate.
Having failed to find a partner who can live up to unrealistic expectations, the
people Katz describes have convinced themselves that their pets love them
unconditionally, understand them better than anyone else, and will never let
them down. In other words, they have projected their emotional desires onto
their pets. Because the animals cannot speak, there is little risk that these
dreams of perfect relationships will be shattered. As Katz puts it, "Loving human
beings is difficult, unpredictable, and often disappointing. Dog love is safer, perhaps more satisfying: Dogs can't betray us, undermine us, tell us they're angry
or bored. Dogs can't leave" (par. 7).

As an interesting exercise, you might want to work through the essay with
your students, counting the number of times Katz uses words like "disturbing,"
"distressing," and "unnerving." Even the humorous pun of "petophilia" raises a
sinister image of inappropriate sexuality. Ask your students, also, to examine
Katz's examples and consider how excessive love of pets might compromise
human relationships. "Sam," for instance, is so smitten with his dog that he has
voluntarily reduced the time he spends socializing with other people, thereby
lowering his chances of finding a human companion. "Jane" has severely isolated herself for the benefit of her dogs. Although Katz is an enthusiastic dog
lover, press your students to identify his underlying argument about love and
pets. *Can* a person love a dog too much?

Interrogating Assumptions

Of the three categories Katz identifies—partner love, victim love, and surrogate love—partner love is the only one that explores an even give and take. It is, essentially, the ideal. Both victim and surrogate love emphasize the benefit for the provider, the feeling of goodwill one gets from caring for another. All three categories work on the assumption that love means being soul mates; in these cases, one soul in the equation neither judges nor abandons the other. It is safe and pure.

Writing about Cultural Practices

This assignment calls for a brief personal essay that questions Katz's cultural critique and applies his insights to students' own experiences. Anybody who has owned a pet should have no problem writing about emotional attachments to animals, but be aware that not all of your students will have had pets. If this is the case, suggest that they write about somebody they know who has a pet; as another option, they might examine the impact *not* having a pet has had on their relationships with other people.

Additional Resources

Film

Dr. Doolittle (1999)   Eddie Murphy plays the famous part of the doctor who can speak to animals.

Old Yeller (1957)   While his father is gone, a young boy bonds with a stray dog and ultimately has to make the devastating decision to put him down.

Web

Crazy Cat Ladies Society, http://www.crazycatladies.org/   The cat lovers on this site work to combat stereotypes about people devoted to their pets.

Date My Pet, http://www.datemypet.com/   This online dating site has the usual pictures of potential matches but also encourages users to post pictures of their pets.

Scott Russell Sanders, **Looking at Women** (p. 329)

This personal and critical essay is grounded in feminist theory and art criticism. Faced with abundant references to challenging academic works and cultural theorists, students may find themselves overwhelmed by the intellectual rigors of "Looking at Women." If theory is important to you, spend some time explaining and discussing the implications of the major ideas that Sanders invokes: John

Berger's exploration of the male gaze in *Ways of Seeing*, for instance; Simone de Beauvoir's concept of the Other in *The Second Sex*; Kate Millet's theories of pornography in *Sexual Politics*. You might ask students to reread and attempt to summarize the passages that Sanders responds to. Astute readers will notice that he embraces these writers' ideas even as he questions them, revealing the complexities and inherent contradictions of sexual theory.

It is important to acknowledge to your students that "Looking at Women" is an unusually challenging essay and that they will need to read it several times to get a firm hold on Sanders's ideas. If you find your students becoming too baffled or frustrated for discussion to be productive, the essay will reward a careful reading that focuses on Sanders's own experiences and thoughtful questions without muddying the waters with theory. Most important for students to comprehend might be Sanders's unattributed concept that sexuality is socially constructed. Students don't need the technical term to grasp Sanders's point that historical precedent, popular culture, and gender politics influence the specifics of desire—as well as how people act on their sexual urges—at least as strongly as biology does. To help them understand this point, draw your students' attention to the personal episodes Sanders describes. Even as an 11-year-old boy, for example, something in him understands that outside influences—the girl's clothing, his friend's leer, and their mothers' disapproval—affect his physical response to the sight of an attractive young girl well before he has matured into a sexual being. Later, as a college student, he smugly resists the objectification of women in *Playboy* centerfolds even as he catches himself doing it to the women he encounters in his life.

Sanders is equally perplexed by the paradox of women's complicity in their own objectification. Boys and men alike are scolded not to stare, enjoined to consider how women might feel about being the subject of their lustful gazes. Yet from a young age, Sanders writes, women "put themselves on display" (par. 16) and take pains to make themselves sexually attractive. Sanders considers several ideas concerning the effects of objectification, from the notion that it dehumanizes both women and the men who view them as less than human, to the belief that it's a matter of biological imperative, to the argument that it can be a source of subversive power for women who choose to use it to their advantage. How should a man look at a woman? Ultimately, Sanders isn't sure.

Although you should encourage thoughtful discussion of these issues in class, your students should not be expected to resolve them; the questions Sanders raises have been the subject of complex intellectual debate for a long time and have yet to be answered to everybody's satisfaction. Try to get students to focus on how ambivalence and paradox affect the role of sexual attraction in romance.

Interrogating Assumptions

Sanders's ambivalence about sexual attraction is a central theme of "Looking at Women." On a physical level, he is as subject to it as anyone else, but on an intellectual level he can't help but question his own motives. How emotionally meaningful can lust be, he wonders, if it is simultaneously driven by biology and shaped by external influences?

Writing about Cultural Practices

For students to get the most out of this assignment, have them read the third chapter of John Berger's *Ways of Seeing*, as *ReMix* is asking them to apply the groundbreaking theorist's approach to Western art to online dating photographs. Without firsthand knowledge of Berger's methodology, students will be at a disadvantage. Consider distributing photocopies or displaying overhead some of the more compelling sections of Berger's classic work, particularly the introduction to chapter 3 and his discussion of nudes in the artistic tradition. Students might discover on their own that the "men act and [the] women appear" (Berger 47), but they'll find themselves more engaged with the project if they have a theoretical hook on which to hang their analyses. At the very least, point them to paragraph 28 of "Looking at Women," which summarizes Berger's theory.

Additional Resources

Nonfiction

Simone de Beauvoir, *The Second Sex* (1952)   A predecessor to the feminist movement, Beauvoir looks at historical constructions of women as "the Other," or as characterized by lacking.

John Berger, *Ways of Seeing* (1972)   Berger begins his discussion with the tendency of vision to dominate our other senses. Chapters 3 and 7, in particular, suggest ways of evaluating images of women in art and advertising.

Kate Millett, *Sexual Politics* (1969)   Millet's influential study of misogyny provided a foundation for radical feminism.

Film

In the Company of Men (1997)   Writer and director Neil LaBute portrays two corporate types who conceive a plan to seduce a deaf woman as a cruel joke.

Benedict Carey, **The Brain in Love** (p. 341)

Summarizing the results of a handful of scientific and psychological studies, Benedict Carey offers some interesting analysis about the biology of romantic attraction. As he explains, the early stages of romance correlate with a spike in levels of dopamine and norepinephrine in the human brain, causing feelings of euphoria similar to a drug-induced high. Those physical feelings lead many to overlook or reinterpret a beloved's flaws, thus serving a biological purpose:

Studies show that idealizing one's partner increases the chances that a romantic relationship will endure over time. In many ways, "The Brain in Love" offers scientific evidence to support the popular assumption that lust and love are the same thing.

On its own, Carey's article might not be very revelatory for students, especially those who have learned to interpret scientific findings as inviolable truths. Although the author does imply that not all researchers agree with the findings he reports, students who read this article will likely conclude that romance is a biological drive and leave it at that. To encourage critical thinking among your students, then, "The Brain in Love" might best be taught in conjunction with Laura Kipnis's "Against Love" and Scott Russell Sanders's "Looking at Women." Carey's piece poses possible biological answers for the cultural questions raised by those writers, while Kipnis and Sanders offer plausible explanations that complicate Carey's assertions.

Start by making sure that students understand the distinction between sexual and romantic attraction. Carey is not arguing that physical chemistry is biologically driven but rather that the urge to find and commit to a life partner is. Although he reports on *how* neurological reactions are put into process by the initial stages of romance, he does not attempt to speculate *why* those reactions seem to be wired into our brains. Encourage your students to take up this question themselves. What biological purpose might be served by romantically induced feelings of euphoria? Evolutionarily speaking, why might humans be driven to commitment? What are the cultural and social implications of the researchers' findings? Note that Andrew Sullivan raises and attempts to answer some of these questions in his essay "The 'He' Hormone," reprinted in chapter 1.

Writing about Cultural Practices

Both of the projects that follow Carey's article encourage students to approach scientific research with a critical eye.

Social scientists and medical researchers often complain that journalists tend to present research findings out of context, distorting or overstating the implications of their results in the process. For the first assignment, then, encourage your students to research not only the studies Carey cites, but also to look for peer responses to the findings (a simple Google search of the authors' names will turn up some criticism). They may be surprised to find just how contentious scientific interpretations can be. Note that because Carey offers so little context for the research he mentions, students may have a hard time finding the appropriate articles; you may want to give them the bibliographic information provided below.

If the first project seems too clinical or intimidating for nonscience majors, the second one is more playful but just as challenging. To further ground students' understanding, you might refer them to Robert J. Sternberg's book *Psychology of Love.* Even without a thorough overview of his theory, however, the relationship chart mapped out in the textbook should provide enough context for students to analyze fictional relationships. Students might notice, too, that Sternberg's classification meshes with the assumptions outlined in the chapter's introduction: "Intimacy" is analogous to the idea of soul mates; "passion" is analogous to the idea of sexual chemistry; and "decision/commitment" invokes the idea that love lasts forever. As the assignment and the theory on which it is based suggest, popular assumptions about love and romance unavoidably overlap with and complicate each other. The most successful analyses, therefore, will integrate concepts that may at first seem incompatible.

Additional Resources

Nonfiction

Helen Fisher, *Why We Love* (2004)   Citing anthropological and biological research, Fisher makes a case that love is largely chemical.

Robert J. Sternberg, *Cupid's Arrow: The Course of Love through Time* (1998) Sternberg analyzes love in terms of three main aspects: intimacy, passion, and commitment.

Film

Forces of Nature (1999)   It seems that the whole world is conspiring to keep the hero, Ben Affleck, from marrying his fiancée and to push him toward a free-spirited fellow traveler, played by Sandra Bullock.

CLUSTERED READINGS: FOCUS ON THE WEDDING

Caitlin Leffel, **The Look of Love: Wedding Announcements** (p. 347)

New York Times, **Announcement: Victoria Dunn and Terrance Jones** (p. 349)

New York Times, **Announcement: Daniel Gross and Steven Goldstein** (p. 352)

Caitlin Leffel's analysis of the evolution of the *New York Times*'s "Weddings and Celebrations" section assumes a familiarity with the newspaper that your students may not have. Unless they're regular readers of the paper, they probably won't understand Leffel's characterizations of the elite, impossibly accomplished couples whose marriages the *Times* sees fit to print. You might consider, therefore, sharing some additional samples from "Weddings and Celebrations," easily photocopied or accessed online (registration is free). After glancing through a few announcements, students will more readily recognize that the *Times* focuses on society weddings, not the unions of average people. Even within such a rarefied population, however, published wedding announcements inadvertently reflect changing assumptions about modern relationships.

As Leffel points out, the couples getting married in America look different from what they looked liked several decades ago. They are older, perhaps, or the same sex, like the two couples portrayed in the sample announcements. They might be interracial, interdenominational, or intergenerational. The brides are now usually as accomplished, if not more so, than the grooms. Previous marriages are common for both spouses. Spend some time with your students cataloging the modern aspects of both relationships described in the two sample announcements. That the couples defy traditional assumptions—Gross and Goldstein are both men, and Dunn and Jones are significantly older than most newlyweds—will be immediately apparent. But push your students to look further. By reading with a close eye, students might notice, for example, the number of divorces related to the Dunn/Jones marriage, the use of personal ads in the Gross/Goldstein union, religious traditions that fall outside the Protestant majority, cohabitation arrangements, and hesitant family acceptance of both relationships, among other things. As your students examine the announcements, ask them to compose a critical comparison of the articles themselves, looking for information that appears standard to both as well as what details are included for one but not the other. Despite the nontraditional aspects of these two weddings, what cultural assumptions seem to endure in how weddings are described?

Every week, the *Times* highlights an unusually interesting or newsworthy wedding among the standard announcements. After your students examine the Dunn/Jones and Gross/Goldstein stories, you might want to point out that the former is not, in fact, one of the formulaic announcements that Leffel describes, but rather a featured "Vows" article from the *New York Times*'s "Weddings and Celebrations" section. Press your students to consider the implications of this editorial choice. Why, do they suppose, did the *Times* decide that a videoconference ceremony was enough of a novelty to merit special attention but that one of the earliest gay civil unions—indeed, the first one to be chronicled by the paper—was not? What does that decision reveal about the purpose of wedding announcements? About American culture in general?

Interrogating Assumptions

The emphasis in the sample announcements is less on the women's and men's roles in the marriages than on their roles as professionals and members of society. Gone are the days when the male partner was typically the sole breadwinner in the family, and these announcements are careful to include the woman's professional name, which may or may not be her married name. Both partners in the union are likely to be equally accomplished, and the *Times* is not hesitant to cover these accomplishments equally and in detail.

Writing about Cultural Practices

This assignment extends students' analysis of the clustered readings to examples from their own community. Encourage them to build upon the ideas discussed in class and to explore any revelations or questions that the discussion may have raised for them. If, however, any students disagree with classroom consensus, encourage them to use this project to argue for alternative interpretations of the cultural meanings of wedding announcements.

Students should expect to gather at least ten samples, half of them from a couple of decades ago and half of them current; announcements with photographs will be more fruitful than straight text. Stress that comparing older announcements to current ones is essential to the success of this project. Actually seeing the contrast between, and the enduring similarities of, newspaper norms over time will be more intriguing than trudging through recent announcements alone. Differences over time will also help students better recognize the cultural assumptions that pervade weddings. Depending on the location of your campus and on where students grew up, however, archives of local papers may be difficult to access. Often, but not always, a town or college library will have back issues on microforms. If old announcements are unavailable or inaccessible, allow students to choose a city or national newspaper with easily accessible archives, such as the *New York Times* or the *Chicago Tribune*. Another option would be to reframe the assignment as a family-history project. If students have access to clipped announcements of their siblings', parents', and grandparents' weddings, for example, they might be able to combine a visual and textual analysis of the announcements with compelling information about the couples themselves.

Additional Resources

Nonfiction

Bambi Cantrell and Skip Cohen, *The Art of Wedding Photography: Professional Techniques with Style* (2000)   This book explains conventions and trends in wedding photography. Among Cantrell and Cohen's tips: Focus on the bride because she's the one who's been playing "wedding" since she was a little girl.

Television

Sex and the City, "The Catch"   In this episode from the show's final season, Charlotte's wedding nears and she experiences anxiety about her *New York Times* announcement. She is horrified when the photo appears with an ink blob on it.

Web

New York Times, "Weddings and Celebrations," http://www.nytimes.com/ pages/ fashion/weddings/index.html   You can see recent announcements, as well as archives, on the *New York Times* site.

USA Bride, http://www.usabride.com/wedplan/a_inv_word.html   While invitation wording was once standard, social changes have made the invitation harder to write. This site gives samples for a number of scenarios.

Mixing Words and Images:
Creating an Alternative Valentine (p. 354)

As a Christian holiday, St. Valentine's Day was first celebrated at the end of the sixth century BCE. Its origins are murky (one legend has it that St. Valentine defied a Roman wartime decree forbidding marriage), but the holiday seems to have started as a combination fertility ritual and matchmaking festival. The modern practice of sending love notes dates to the seventeenth or eighteenth century. In America, the first commercial valentines were printed in the late 1840s (the first cards were lacy, but risqué images were also popular during the Victorian era). Gift giving wasn't added to the tradition until the mid-twentieth century; the diamond industry started encouraging men to purchase jewelry for their valentines in the 1980s. Although the Catholic Church removed Valentine's Day from its calendar of holy days in 1969, Americans continue to recognize this traditional day of romance and courtship. According to the Greeting Card Association, more than a billion valentines are mailed in the United States each year; 85 percent of them are purchased by women.

Probably no other American holiday spawns as much ambivalence as Valentine's Day does. Although the holiday is widely celebrated, people without mates tend to resent either the pressure to find a partner or the ubiquitous reminder that they don't have one; many couples, in turn, find the holiday artificial, overly commercial, and decidedly *not* romantic. The Bittersweets candies pictured in the assignment are targeted at the former group, but students might just as easily produce an alternative valentine for new or committed couples. They might also want to consider the cut-out cards typically distributed among schoolchildren. The trick will be for students to move beyond simple cynicism to create an image that poses serious questions or makes a thoughtful criticism of an assumption surrounding romance.

If you're teaching the chapter at any time other than February, students may have some difficulty finding sample cards to start with. If you find this to be the case, inform them that most electronic greeting-card sites keep their valentines options up at all times; American Greetings also posts images of their cards online throughout the year. Point your students to the old-fashioned valentine pictured on page 290; they should be able to locate additional images of antique cards by searching the Web for "vintage valentines." Have them check the library as well; several collections of vintage cards have been published.

Remember that this assignment combines both visual and written components. Be sure students understand that they should not only describe and critique their image, but also ponder the origins and implications of the assumption their valentine questions.

Connecting to Culture: Suggestions for Writing (p. 356)

The writing assignments that conclude the chapter offer students an opportunity to synthesize the ideas they've encountered in the readings and to make some conclusions about the assumptions outlined in the chapter introduction.

What Is Love Now? A Dialogue Essay on Romance

Some students immediately take to dialogue essays and thrive on their unconventional approach; others find them hopelessly strange as a writing project and never catch on. Because the genre for this project may feel unnatural for some students, consider assigning it as one of two or more options. Given sufficient guidance and flexibility, however, most students should be able to produce workable dialogues. The most important thing to explain to them is that the quoted passages from several readings must speak to each other. It's not enough to simply patch together a series of quotations on a topic. They'll need to choose a focus ahead of time and scour the readings for potential dialogue, prepared all the while to adjust their focus as they find promising passages. Students will likely succeed on this assignment if you can provide them with some models of successful dialogue essays, perhaps from your own portfolio, from previous students, or from published works.

"Are You Hot or Not?": Investigating Attraction

This assignment asks students to draw on an idea explained in a chapter reading to develop their own theory about one aspect of romance—attraction. Because both Sanders and Carey synthesize the work of other writers, students would do well to track down and review the original sources of the ideas they encounter in their essays (for a bibliographic list of these sources, see the manual entries for "Looking at Women," pp. 90–92, and "The Brain in Love," pp. 92–94). Student papers should begin by summarizing the theory (or theories) of their choice, but the purpose of the assignment is to expand on a writer's ideas to develop and test an original theory about attraction. Although the assignment doesn't explicitly call for visual analysis, student responses will be richer and more thoughtful if you encourage them to include descriptions and criticisms of several images from the dating sites they examine. Rather than simply presenting a theory, in other words, students should use their theories to analyze multiple pictures intended to attract romantic partners.

Is TV Love like Real-life Love? A Critical Analysis

This project encourages students to test ideas from the chapter by applying them to examples from popular culture, specifically to romantic relationships portrayed on television. If your students haven't already read it, you might want to inform them that David Sedaris's "The End of the Affair" (p. 272) offers a useful model of the kind of criticism the assignment calls for (although they don't need to imitate his style if they don't want to). In addition to describing two relationships of their choice, students should be careful to consider how those relationships reinforce or reject assumptions about romance.

Interrogating Assumptions: What's Love Got to Do with It?

The most formal of the writing projects in this chapter, this final assignment calls for a text-based comparative analysis that synthesizes ideas from the chapter and several individual readings. To ensure coherence, encourage students to select readings that are closely related thematically as well as in the way they address assumptions about tradition. If you've assigned any of the Interrogating Assumptions or Connecting to Another Reading questions that follow some of the selections in the chapter, allow your students to use their responses as starting points for their drafts. A successful student essay will posit a thesis about one of the assumptions and use the readings to support it, rather than simply compare and contrast several selections.

5 Entertainment

... or, why are we so bored?

Entertainment is a powerful force in American culture. Advertisers use humor and drama to sell their products; politicians throw galas and host concerts to gather support; entertainers send political messages at awards ceremonies; churches create elaborate multimedia productions to build and preach to their congregations. Conversations at social gatherings frequently turn to reviews of the latest blockbuster movie, discussions of a plot twist in last week's episode of *Desperate Housewives,* or comments like "There's a *Simpsons* episode about that." Those who don't understand a reference or share enthusiasm for the latest trend might feel like outcasts. As the readings in this chapter argue and demonstrate, cultural forms of amusement convey subtle and not-so-subtle messages about what a society values, what behaviors and attitudes are acceptable, and what changes are possible.

Whether manifested as a commercial product or a personal endeavor, popular entertainment has a strong influence on every other aspect of culture explored in the chapters of *ReMix*: Shared cultural references affect our understandings of personal identity, community belonging, tradition, romance, nature, and technology. As a result, this chapter can productively be taught in conjunction with any other topic in the reader, depending on your own and your students' interests. In some ways, assumptions about entertainment will be the easiest for students to recognize and question; most are media savvy and will implicitly understand that nothing about popular culture can be taken for granted. At the same time, Americans are so bombarded with mass entertainment in every aspect of their lives that it can be difficult to examine from a critical distance.

Before you have students read the chapter introduction, you may want to explore, as a class or through a preliminary journal assignment, what assumptions they currently hold about their own experiences with entertainment and amusement. Brainstorm as a group what "entertainment" is, who produces it and why, and how it is consumed. What do your students do for fun? Why do they enjoy it? Do they pursue any particular forms of entertainment as a way of fitting in with others, or does their idea of fun distinguish them from the masses? How does popular culture affect their sense of who they are? The Examining the Everyday assignment that opens the chapter will help them explore this last question without putting them on the defensive. The simple act of compiling a list of songs that speak to who they are will encourage students to question how popular culture has influenced them. And as they answer questions about why the songs are so significant for them, students will begin to recognize that the web connecting culture, community, tradition, romance, and identity is tangled indeed.

Because the central assumptions outlined in the chapter's introduction form the basis for analyzing the chapter's readings, spend some time discussing them in class. Use the questions that follow each discussion of an assumption to explore the concept with your students. You might want to ask your students whether they agree or disagree with the outlined assumptions and what other assumptions about entertainment they can identify. Discuss with your class, also, how these assumptions function in American culture. Who holds them? What purposes do they serve? Are they helpful or harmful? And how do students see them played out in their personal lives and in the world around them?

All of the readings in this chapter question one or several of the three main assumptions outlined in the introduction—entertainment is just for fun; entertainment is merely a reflection of culture; entertainment is a personal choice. Pop-culture critic Adam Sternbergh analyzes one of Britney Spears's letters to her fans and a few of her videos to question how the entertainment industry manipulates the cultural meanings of sexuality and female autonomy. Similarly, film scholar David Sterritt and actor Samuel L. Jackson explore how racial stereotypes in movies distort American perceptions of minority cultures. Several readings—"Virtual Dictionary" (p. 438), "The Unreal World" (p. 442), and "Queer Eye: Searching for a Real Gay Man" (p. 449)—analyze the cultural meanings of one of today's most popular mass-entertainment formats: reality television. Journalists Katie Roiphe and Pete Rojas examine issues of plagiarism and originality surrounding the cult of celebrity and the growing popularity of do-it-yourself music. Cultural critic Alain de Botton analyzes several historical cartoons to develop a theory that comedy is a subversive tool for critiquing social and power elites. In his overview of kitschy tourist destinations, historian John Margolies suggests that these uniquely American amusements reflect a range of the country's attitudes about race and class as well as leisure. Two readings explore how local and federal government use censorship to control the working classes: David Nasaw's "The Pernicious 'Moving Picture' Abomination" (p. 411) evaluates efforts to shut down nickelodeon shows in the early twentieth century, while Ira Glass's "Howard and Me" (p. 432) explores similar dynamics in objections to the *Howard Stern Show*. Capping off the chapter, Sarah Vowell's humorous personal narrative about a simple arcade game reveals the social benefits of pointless fun.

Nonfiction

Michael Denning, *The Cultural Front: The Laboring of American Culture in the Twentieth Century* (1997)   Denning's study of the political uses of popular culture focuses on Communist sympathizers in the 1930s and '40s.

Radio

"Big Churches Use Technology to Branch Out"   Jennifer Ludden's report, which first aired on *All Things Considered* in August 2005, investigates how "megachurches" use entertainment to deliver religious messages. Audio of the show is available at http://www.npr.org/templates/story/story.php ?storyId=4788676.

Web

E! Online, http://www.eonline.com   E! is a television network dedicated to observing the entertainment industry. Their website features fashion criticism, gossip, and celebrity profiles.

Adam Sternbergh, **Britney Spears: The Pop Tart in Winter** (p. 371)

Adam Sternbergh's essay asks students to reflect on Britney Spears as an example of how female sexuality is presented and sold by the pop-music industry. Since the MTV debut of "Baby One More Time," music critics and cultural commentators have voiced alarm at how the former Mouseketeer—whose primary audience initially consisted of preadolescent girls—juxtaposes childhood innocence and adult sexuality. To a great extent, the concern has been that Spears's carefully constructed image, not to mention her sexually aggressive lyrics, fetishizes the sexualization of children. At the same time, it encourages young fans to emulate Britney's sex-kitten persona without understanding its implications. As Sternbergh explains, Spears has consistently responded to such criticisms by insisting that she is not the person she appears to be, that she is an innocent victim of the calculated image projected by her "advisors."

Certainly, that line of defense is evident in her October 2004 letter to fans, which students can read in its entirety at britneyspears.com or through a link for chapter 5 at the book's companion site (bedfordstmartins.com/remix). Students may notice that Spears makes casual references to an overbearing stage mother and to greedy corporate handlers who force a young girl to go against her best interests. They may need some prodding, however, to recognize how Spears invokes aspects of her media persona even as she claims she wants no part of it. You might want to call their attention to her use of the words "blonde," "girl," and "icon," for example, as well as her overt references to her latest single. As

Sternbergh points out, Spears has made a career of artfully combining virtue and disingenuity. Perhaps the best way to illustrate his point is to spend some time with your students deconstructing the webpage on which Spears's missive appears. The visual context of the letter is telling. Ask your students to consider not only the photographs but also the links to press articles, personal information, and opportunities to purchase music and Britney paraphernalia. Spears's argument that she wants a break from publicity is surrounded by self-promotion. How, you might ask your students, would her message have been affected if she published it somewhere else?

Interrogating Assumptions

Spears suggests that although she has no choice in how her image is constructed and presented to her fans, her audience has a choice in how it responds to that image. But as Sternbergh points out, her line of defense is disingenuous. It's impossible to separate her music from her publicity; the one has never existed independently of the other. While Americans may be able to avoid listening to Britney Spears's music or watching her videos, anybody who shops for groceries is bombarded with magazine headlines at the checkout counter. Some might argue, as well, that Spears's success as a pop star has always been contingent on the publicity stunts and personal choices that have landed her in the press and kept her in the spotlight. The same elements that are used to construct Spears's sexual ingenue persona are employed to manipulate the meanings of that image for her audience.

Writing about Cultural Practices

It has become a truism of American popular culture that child stars are likely doomed to self-destruction. Young actors and musicians seem to be aware of how many of their predecessors succumbed to drugs, alcohol, criminal behavior, even suicide, and yet they pursue fame nonetheless. This assignment asks students to explore the dynamics of this apparent contradiction. What drives young people to seek stardom? And how does achieving it affect them?

Students will be most successful in their analyses if they do some research to support their interpretations of child-star imagery. Biographies, autobiographies, and published or broadcast interviews will likely prove fruitful, although students should be careful to consider the purpose and objectivity of the sources they find. With that in mind, you should discourage them from relying on fan sites for their information. Note, too, that although the assignment implies that students should focus on contemporary stars, examining the celebrity of actors or musicians from past decades offers the added benefit of considering how their lives, and their stardom, changed as they matured.

Additional Resources

Television

Britney and Kevin: Chaotic   Following in the footsteps of Jessica Simpson and Nick Lachey, Britney and her new husband became the focus of a reality TV show, but they received disappointing ratings.

Web

Britney Spears official website, http://www.britneyspears.com/   You can click on "Love B," Britney's blog, to read further messages to her fans.

Adam Sternbergh's Archive, http://newyorkmetro.com/nymag/10222/   In this archive of entertainment columns for *New York* magazine, you can read about, among other things, medical reality shows, a TV network designed for the gay community, and the criteria for choosing news anchors.

Katie Roiphe, **Profiles Encouraged** (p. 376)

Celebrity profiles, or articles about popular entertainers, are themselves a form of entertainment. Roiphe's overview of the genre offers a model critical analysis of a cultural artifact. If any of your students have been having trouble writing critical analyses of their own, you can use this essay to review how good cultural criticism is researched, organized, and argued.

Much as a literary critic might analyze a work of fiction, Roiphe carefully examines several celebrity profiles to identify the components that are common to most articles in the genre. The "narrative arc" starts by presenting the star as a regular person, progresses to fawning over the qualities that make him or her special, and concludes with awe and wonder. Stock phrases are used to describe physical features and character traits. Other components include the disdain for (and similarity to) tabloid gossip, overused rhetorical strategies, and an implication of intimacy between profiler and star. Note how Roiphe produces several examples in the form of quotations to support her analysis.

Make sure that your students recognize that Roiphe doesn't simply establish the components of these magazine articles to prove that "all movie-star profiles are the same" (par. 1). Rather, she uses her observations to argue that the relentless clichés of celebrity profiles reveal something about American culture—that "we are not interested in Winona Ryder, we are interested in fame" (15). Press your students to interpret what Roiphe means by this. She argues that it is not the celebrities themselves who are important; what captures the American imagination is a platonic ideal of celebrity. And if fame inspires worship, the celebrity profile is a religious ritual. In other words, to acknowledge the individuality of a particular star would be to destroy the fantasy of stardom.

Interrogating Assumptions

Roiphe's purpose with this essay is to dispute the assumption that entertainment is just for fun, by assessing the cultural meanings of one popular form of entertainment. Although she seems to accept the assumption that entertainment is simply a reflection of culture (she writes in par. 2 that the journalists who produce celebrity profiles are "giving the magazine or the reader or the movie publicists what they want—and nothing more"), Roiphe also suggests that the ritual sameness of the profiles is a by-product of efforts to promote new movies. Fans want to read the same article over and over, she implies, because that's what they've been conditioned to expect.

Writing about Cultural Practices

Primed by Roiphe's close look at celebrity profiles, students will likely enjoy the challenge of writing one that follows the formula she outlines. Rather than relying entirely on Roiphe's overview, however, encourage students to better acquaint themselves with the genre by reading several celebrity profiles, either online or in print. And although your students will be emulating formulaic writing, discourage them from copying any phrases or descriptions outright. (This assignment offers an excellent opportunity to discuss plagiarism and the serious consequences of borrowing another writer's words or ideas without attribution.)

The challenge of writing a celebrity profile is only part of this assignment. Students will use their experience of following the formula to analyze the cultural meanings of celebrity profiles. Their tendency will be to paraphrase Roiphe's points, an intellectual shortcut you'll want them to avoid. You might, therefore, want to explicitly instruct your students not to parrot Roiphe's critique, telling them that, although it's fine to agree with her, you expect them to produce and support theories of their own.

Additional Resources

Nonfiction

Michael Denning, *Mechanic Accents: Dime Novels and Working Class Culture in America* (1987)   Denning analyzes the popularity of dime novels, which provided nineteenth-century readers with their fill of "real-life" struggles and scandals.

Film

Celebrity (1998)   In Woody Allen's look at Hollywood life, Kenneth Branagh plays a divorced man who tries to make a living by writing celebrity profiles while pitching his movie script.

Television

Behind the Music   VH1's take on the celebrity profile follows its own story arc, usually showing the musicians' descent into drugs and despair followed by, in varying degrees, triumphant return.

Radio

The Connection, "Celebrity Worship"   In this show from June 2004, host Judy Swallow speaks to an anthropologist, a psychologist, a journalist, and a fan in an attempt to understand the phenomenon of celebrity worship. Audio is available at http://www.theconnection.org/shows/2004/06/20040607_b _main.asp.

Pete Rojas, **Bootleg Culture** (p. 383)

Neither the practice of appropriating other artists' works nor the question of individual authorship is new. Although bootlegging may take cultural sampling to new extremes, artists have adapted, referred to, satirized, and combined the works of their predecessors and contemporaries for centuries. Early rock-and-roll musicians, for example, repackaged the work of blues artists without acknowledging their sources. The longest running situation comedy of all time, *The Simpsons,* is an endless and multilayered series of references to popular culture, historical events, biblical stories, contemporary politics, and academic debates. Even Shakespeare, widely acknowledged as the most talented creative genius in the history of Western civilization, routinely borrowed plots, characters, and themes from Plutarch and Ovid, who in turn relied heavily on oral tradition and the works of other writers. Indeed, several theorists, notably C. G. Jung and T. S. Eliot, have argued that all creative expressions are inevitably reworkings of previous ideas, that original creation is impossible.

The title of *ReMix* itself is based on the practice of sampling. The book is designed to address the culture that students are a part of—a collaborative, multimedia, cut-and-paste culture. Learning, after all, is a process of combining ideas from multiple sources to establish understanding and inspire new ideas. You may want to ask your students, then, to consider the parallels between musical mash-ups and academic writing. Where does borrowing end and originality begin?

Bootlegging may at first seem like a radical departure from accepted cross-referencing traditions, but Rojas suggests that the distinction lies only in the democratic possibilities created by technology. As more and more people enjoy affordable access to the tools that make it easy to remix the work of traditional artists and to share the results, he argues, those with extensive financial resources are losing their monopoly on the creative process. Rojas presents this as a positive development, but the issue is far from settled. Not only do musicians and representatives of the recording industry struggle with questions of intellectual property and the limits of creative expression, but so do scholars and legal experts. Rather than accepting Rojas's assertions at face value, encourage students to debate the artistic and social merits of downloading and reworking existing songs and films. Some questions you might ask include: Is this practice in fact its own form of creativity? What marks the distinction between borrowing for the purpose of social critique and theft? Who has the stronger claim on published works, the artists who create them or the audience that embraces them? Does protecting copyright hinder creativity?

Writing about Cultural Practices

This unconventional assignment encourages students to experiment with an emerging form of cultural expression. Some members of your class may be uncomfortable at the prospect of sampling published works without permission. You can assure them that copyright laws apply to the *distribution* of unauthorized remixes, not to their creation. Fair use and educational use laws allow students to create a collage from any works they like; they may not, however, legally publish or distribute their end products outside the classroom without obtaining the written permission of every artist (or copyright holder) whose work they've appropriated for their own creative expression. For students without the technical skills or equipment to manipulate sources electronically or audiovisually, remind them that they may create a simple cut-and-paste collage on a sheet of paper. Similarly, don't let students argue that they can't complete this project because they're not talented artists. The technical and aesthetic merits of the final collages are less important than students' experiences creating them. Finally, by producing their own mashes or remixes, students will test Pete Rojas's cultural analysis that bootlegging is a legitimate form of creative expression.

Additional Resources

Nonfiction

Simon Wallis, *Remix: Contemporary Art and Pop Music* (2002)   This catalog accompanied an exhibition of the same name at the Tate Museum in Liverpool, England; it considered the intersections of art and popular music and the use of visual references to previous artworks.

Web

Creative Commons, http://www.creativecommons.org   This nonprofit organization allows artists to publish their creative work with flexible copyrights; they are encouraged to share and remix their audio, visual, and textual pieces. The website for Creative Commons' chairperson, Lawrence Lessig, can be found at http://www.lessig.org/blog.

Get Your Bootleg On, http://www.gybo-v3.co.uk/index.php   This message board contains links to files of mash-up songs.

Nine Inch Nails, http://www.nin.com/   Trent Reznor of Nine Inch Nails has posted multitrack files of a song from the album *With Teeth* so that fans can remix it themselves using music software.

Alain de Botton, **Comedy** (p. 390)

A productive way to begin discussion of de Botton's essay might be to ask your students to bring to class a copy of their favorite print cartoon or to name comedians, movies, or television programs they consider especially funny. Explore with them why certain kinds of humor make them laugh, digging beneath the surface to identify the cultural critiques embedded in the comedy. *Dilbert,* for example, underscores the inhumanity of the modern workplace (and has consequently been banned from some offices); Chris Rock and Dave Chappelle criticize race relations; Jon Stewart routinely lambastes media reporting on nearly every major news event. Even physical comedy, with its pratfalls and distorted faces, often makes critical observations about human frailties, and children's cartoons attempt to teach lessons about how to interact with others.

Anybody who has hurt another person's feelings and insisted that "I was only joking" or asked, "Can't you take a joke?" should be able to recognize that at the heart of humor lies criticism. To help your students grasp de Botton's argument that humor is a tool to critique the powerful, ask them if they can think of any instances in which a member of the elite successfully used humor to make a point about a powerless group. In most cases, such an attempt would result in a backlash against the joker (consider the *New Yorker* cartoon poking fun at the wealthy on p. 396—although the couple are criticizing somebody with no money, the joke is aimed at their pretensions). What, then, is the relationship between humor and power?

Just as people may laugh to avoid crying, comedy offers a way for a society to face its troubles. Although de Botton argues that comedic jabs at the mighty can help bring them down, some students might counter that making jokes discourages dispossessed groups from taking corrective action. Encourage debate on this point, referring students to the second assumption outlined in the chapter introduction (p. 364). Is humor, as de Botton suggests, a catalyst for change, or does it help maintain the status quo by making it more palatable?

Finally, be sure to spend some time in class examining the images that accompany de Botton's essay, considering how they support his cultural critique and questioning how jokes are affected by cultural context. Distanced from the class antagonisms of the Gilded Age, for example, students might not see the humor in Mary Petty's cartoon on page 394. As you determine which cartoons have retained their humor over time and which have not, ask your students how their responses to the jokes undermine or reinforce de Botton's point that humor is a tool for social critique.

Interrogating Assumptions

Explicitly rejecting the idea that entertainment is simply a form of amusement, de Botton suggests that comedy offers a way for people and societies to face painful truths, provides a strategy for alleviating anxiety, and opens opportunities to forge social and political change. Although comedy necessarily reflects the social context out of which it is born, de Botton argues that comics use their art not to reflect cultural realities so much as to reveal injustices and, by doing so, to overcome them.

Writing about Cultural Practices

This project encourages students to apply de Botton's historically grounded theories to an example from contemporary popular culture. If analyzing an entire program seems like too much, suggest that your students limit their inquiry to a single part of the show: the opening monologue, for example, or a skit or an interview. Inform students, as well, that they don't have to analyze one of the talk shows the assignment offers as examples: Equally promising programs include skit shows like *Saturday Night Live* or *Mad TV*, adult-oriented cartoons such as *South Park* and *Family Guy*, and just about anything that airs on Comedy Central, so long as students can identify an explicit political or cultural critique embedded in the program's humor.

Before analyzing a show of their choice, students should work through de Botton's essay, either individually or as a group, to identify his specific arguments about the uses of humor. Successful papers will consider each of de Botton's points as it applies to a televised example, whether writers find themselves agreeing or disagreeing with the philosopher's argument.

Additional Resources

Nonfiction

Ronald K. L. Collins and David M. Skover, *The Trials of Lenny Bruce: The Fall and Rise of an American Icon* (2002) Legal scholars Collins and Skover examine Lenny Bruce's career through the lens of his battles against obscenity charges. Bruce used comedy to challenge American prejudices and inequities.

Sigmund Freud, *Jokes and Their Relationship to the Unconscious* (1960) In this book, Freud suggests that jokes are keys to our deep unconscious anxieties.

Film

Modern Times (1936) Charlie Chaplin, in one of his most famous roles, plays a factory worker driven crazy by the oppressive monotony of his job.

Web

American Humor Studies Association, http://www.americanhumor.org/ Humor studies is a growing academic field. On this site, you can find details about conferences and the journal of the American Humor Studies Association.

John Margolies, **Amazing! Incredible! The Roadside Attraction** (p. 398)

Often dismissed as silly or disparaged as eyesores, roadside attractions—especially those on the brink of ruin—have developed a cultlike following. Grassroots groups and preservation societies across the country have fought to save dilapidated muffler men, demonic clowns, and bizarre folk-art sculptures not simply because they're amusing but because they represent Americana.

In their heyday, roadside attractions were essentially elaborate marketing tools. Other genres of roadside attractions followed on the heels of those designed to bring new customers to established businesses. Margolies classifies several overlapping types, including the natural wonder, the spectacle for its own sake, the theme park, the animal sideshow, the quirky museum, the (deceptive) mysterious phenomenon, and the collection of folk art—most of them deriving their income from admission fees and souvenir sales. Students who haven't traveled outside of the United States may not realize that the attractions Margolies describes are uniquely American. You may want to ponder with your students why these quirky sites would have emerged in North America but not in someplace like Europe, Asia, or Africa. What is it about American culture that could have fostered the proliferation of unnecessary businesses and kitschy entertainment?

Interrogating Assumptions

In the realm of the roadside attraction, novelty provides its own entertainment. But as the cultural history of these sites suggests, roadside entrepreneurs shrewdly fabricated self-conscious silliness, manipulating the tedium of long-distance driving for easy profit. Some cynics would argue as well that the artificiality and tackiness of roadside attractions are a perfect reflection of American culture as a whole. And public battles over the fate of surviving sites raise the question of whether entertainment is a choice: How can a person possibly ignore an 85-foot dinosaur?

Writing about Cultural Practices

Because this assignment gives students the opportunity to work as a cultural anthropologist, encourage them to visit a site personally if it's at all possible, perhaps by arranging a class field trip. Students will learn as much by observing other visitors as they will by exploring the site itself. Many communities have some kind of roadside attraction nearby, whether it's a major destination or a local restaurant's bizarre mascot. The biggest obstacle to a physical visit might be the admission fee, if there is one. If this is the case, consider calling ahead and inquiring about reduced rates or complimentary tickets. The Web alternative offered in the textbook should be pursued only as a last resort.

Before students embark on their mission, explain to them what goes into a successful field observation. They should expect to take careful notes on the physical site, writing down detailed descriptions of the location, any billboards or road signs that lead up to it, the attraction itself, any souvenir kiosks, and its immediate surroundings. It would be a good idea to bring a camera and take plenty of photographs, which students can examine at their leisure and include as exhibits with their analyses. They should pay attention to their own responses to the attraction and record their thoughts as they tour it. Ideally, students should try to talk to a few other people they encounter at the attraction, asking why they've visited and what they think of it. In fact, if students plan to visit the site, they might want to prepare a list of interview questions and bring a tape recorder, keeping in mind that they need to ask permission before recording any interviews. If possible, students should also interview a docent or guide.

As they write their analyses, students should consider both how the site promotes itself and how visitors respond to it, noting disparities between intention and interpretation and venturing explanations for the differences. A successful paper will describe the site and its cultural context in enough detail so that somebody who has never been there can picture it. It will also make an attempt at answering the question posed in the assignment: "What does this attraction reveal about the purpose or impact of 'amusements' in American life?"

Additional Resources

Nonfiction

Doug Kirby, *The New Roadside America: The Modern Traveler's Guide to the Wild and Wonderful World of America's Tourist Attractions* (1992)   A guide to the country's roadside attractions, Kirby's book is arranged by theme. Travelers can find sightseeing options relating to Elvis, alligators, or pyramids.

Mark Moran and Marc Sceurman, *Weird U.S.: Your Travel Guide to America's Local Legends and Best Kept Secrets* (2004)   The authors collect local lore from around the country, focusing on the occult and the uncanny.

Fiction

Tom Robbins, *Another Roadside Attraction* (1990)   In this novel, a roadside hot-dog stand with a flea circus takes on religious significance with the arrival of a mysterious corpse.

Web

Roadside America, http://www.roadsideamerica.com   Visitors to this site can post updates about their own visits to roadside attractions.

David Nasaw, **The Pernicious "Moving Picture" Abomination** (p. 411)

To fully understand the phenomenon described in this essay, students will likely need an explanation of what a nickelodeon theater was. These ubiquitous storefront theaters were nothing like the multiplexes modern moviegoers are familiar with. Patronized almost exclusively by largely immigrant laborers and their families, nickelodeons typically filled the street-level space of a neighborhood shop converted for the purpose of showing motion pictures. These silent films were about 15 or 20 minutes long and accompanied by live piano. Most popular were melodramas, crime stories, adventures, stop-action sequences (such as a building demolition), and slapstick comedies. Although some critics bemoaned the passivity of movie audiences as compared to theater audiences, nickelodeon patrons typically responded loudly to the action on the screen and interacted with each other during the show. The small rooms—which might have been about 1,500 square feet and seated fewer than 200 people on average—were boisterous environments, filled with noise, smoke, and activity.

David Nasaw's research provides a historical perspective for contemporary controversies surrounding popular entertainment. Although this excerpt from *Going Out: The Rise and Fall of Public Amusements* focuses on criticisms of nickelodeon theaters in the early twentieth century, similar charges were leveled against live theater in the late nineteenth century and against novels in the eighteenth. Then, as now, critics rested their arguments on the assumption that the general public (women, immigrants, and children especially) is incapable of applying critical thought to the amusements provided for them, that they'll accept and act upon whatever values they are exposed to.

Nasaw suggests but doesn't explore the point that the only values deemed acceptable by antivice crusaders were (and are) defined by a white, middle class, protestant worldview. Most nickelodeon patrons, by necessity, lived in deplorably unsanitary tenements and worked for meager pay in dangerously unhealthy environments. Students might recognize that antivice crusaders weren't trying to reform moving pictures so much as they were trying to reform the people who patronized them. Rather than attack the housing and labor environments that posed serious risks to the health and perceived morality of the working class, reformers targeted their entertainment. The reformers' goal, however, was to maintain social and political control of mass entertainment by whatever means possible.

Interrogating Assumptions

Like many of their middle and upper class contemporaries, antivice crusaders of the early twentieth century assumed that working class and immigrant audiences were passive consumers of entertainment who would absorb whatever moral values were presented to them. Alarmed by the content of the most popular types of short films, reformers believed that tales of depravity and images of violence would inevitably teach viewers to emulate what they saw on the screen. They did not consider that viewers might find such material amusing for its own sake; rather, they believed that entertainment's purpose was to offer civic and religious lessons to its audience. Personal choice, from this perspective, was a dangerous thing, because the lower classes could not be trusted to make the right decisions for themselves.

Writing about Cultural Practices

This research project—essentially an investigation of the assumption that entertainment is a matter of personal choice—asks students to formally analyze the arguments proffered by opponents of a popular form of modern entertainment. Although one or two secondary analyses of a controversy, such as magazine or newspaper articles or a televised report, might help ground their approach, students should focus their analysis on primary-source documents. You may, therefore, want to spend some time explaining the difference between primary and secondary works and giving students some leads for finding appropriate documents to analyze. Consider scheduling an on-site tutorial with a research librarian; most are delighted to introduce students to the college's facilities and show them how to identify and obtain promising sources.

Encourage students, as well, to familiarize themselves with the entertainment medium under debate. If they are exploring concerns regarding gay characters in children's stories, for example, they should read the book or books targeted for censorship. If they are researching debates over violent video games, they should spend at least an hour playing one of the games in question. If they are considering arguments about racist films (see the paired essays by David Sterritt and Samuel L. Jackson on pp. 425–30), they should view at least one of the movies that have stirred controversy. If they are interested in radio censorship (see Ira Glass's "Howard and Me" on p. 432), they should listen to one of the programs that have come under FCC scrutiny.

Finally, keep in mind that it's possible that student writers will support some of the arguments they find for restricting a given form of entertainment. Although you may certainly require that they critically analyze those arguments, assure students that you will not penalize them for their opinions one way or the other.

Additional Resources

Nonfiction

Q. David Bowers, *Nickelodeon Theatres and Their Music* (1986)   This history of nickelodeons is constructed of primary documents: photographs, advertisements, and articles from contemporary periodicals.

Lawrence Levine, *High Brow/Low Brow: The Emergence of Cultural Hierarchy in America* (1988)   Observing changes in Americans' attitudes to popular entertainment, Levine argues that the distinction between high and low art forms emerged in the late nineteenth century and that the division is being eroded in contemporary life.

Kathy Peiss, *Cheap Amusements: Working Women and Leisure in Turn-of-the-Century New York* (1986)   Peiss looks at nickelodeons as one of the leisure activities open to women of the working class.

PAIRED READINGS: FOCUS ON HOLLYWOOD

David Sterritt, **Face of an Angel** (p. 425)
Samuel L. Jackson, **In Character** (p. 428)

Taken together, Sterritt's and Jackson's essays reveal how Hollywood continues to struggle with the problem of racism. Although overtly racist portrayals that were once the norm have become rare, and although race-neutral roles are becoming more common, both writers argue that more subtle forms of racism have taken hold of Hollywood. Sterritt suggests that the recent movie trend of black "angel" characters, although well intentioned and on the surface a positive development, perpetuates a cultural belief that African Americans are either less than human or, as spiritual guides, beyond human. And from Jackson's perspective, as long as mainstream audiences expect and pay to see white actors in most roles, Hollywood will be unwilling to risk investing in movies that challenge those prejudices.

You may find that some of your students are frustrated by the criticisms launched in these essays, feeling (if not daring to say out loud) that the writers take their examples too far or that they expect too much from the movies. If you encounter this kind of resistance, use it to explore the assumptions that undergird both perspectives. For Sterritt and Jackson, big-budget entertainment has a responsibility not only to reflect culture but also to influence it. Those who would argue that it's not Hollywood's job to restructure American race relations may also believe that entertainment is nothing more than a reflection of culture and should be commended for evolving as much as it has.

If students doubt that movies can change popular attitudes about race, you may want to expand on Sterritt's allusion to D. W. Griffith's *Birth of a Nation* (1915), probably the most disturbing example of racist filmmaking in American history. Based on Thomas Dixon, Jr.'s widely read 1905 novel, *The Clansman: An Historical Romance of the Ku Klux Klan,* the film was created explicitly as a piece of racial propaganda and was intended to fuel animosity toward African Americans, whose growing political power was deeply troubling to many white politicians in the South. The movie did everything Dixon and Griffith had

hoped—and more. Several movie audiences, horrified by the animalistic violence against white women perpetrated by the movie's black villain, rioted after
showings. Historian Glenda Gilmore credits the movie with inspiring the founding of the second Ku Klux Klan. Other viewers were horrified by the movie's
overt racism and used the film as a catalyst for their efforts to promote reform.
Birth of a Nation perpetuated the myth that black men were raping white women
in growing numbers, a myth that created a panic and was consciously used to
justify lynching and the political repression of African Americans.

If the movies can be used to reinforce cultural evils, Sterritt and Jackson
imply, surely they can be used to promote cultural good. Ask your students to
compare the writers' ideas about what Hollywood should do to correct its racial
flaws. Sterritt suggests that filmmakers have an obligation to tackle racial issues
directly, using their movies to address questions of racism and inequity in
American culture. Jackson, on the other hand, concludes by suggesting that the
best way to accelerate the production of films that feature nonwhite characters in
mainstream roles is to form nonwhite production and distribution companies.
You might want to ask your students, Is there a middle ground between these
perspectives? How can the problem be solved?

Interrogating Assumptions

Both Sterritt and Jackson reject the idea that entertainment is just for fun. Each
of them examines recent Hollywood films in an effort to uncover the cultural
attitudes that they project and reinforce. At the same time, they accept, to some
degree, the assumption that entertainment is a reflection of culture. Jackson, for
example, notes that it is a reflection of American progress that nonwhite actors
now have access to roles that move beyond racial and ethnic stereotypes. As producers' experiences and attitudes change, he explains, their movies reflect the
evolution of cultural attitudes toward race. Both writers, however, would like to
see filmmakers take a more active role in shaping, rather than merely mirroring,
American race relations.

Writing about Cultural Practices

This assignment gives students an opportunity to look below the surface of a
popular form of entertainment and discover what it reveals about an aspect of
American culture. To give students an interpretive handle, consider limiting
their options to one of the movies that Sterritt discusses in "Face of an Angel."
Although he offers compelling and valid insights for each of the movies he mentions, others who see the same films may come away with very different conclusions. Having an interpretation against which to measure their own responses
will give students a useful starting place for their own analyses.

If you'd rather move away from Sterritt's "angel" thesis, encourage students
to read several reviews of a movie that they've seen and are interested in writing
about. In this case, too, exposure to different opinions will help to spark students'

own ideas. Writing about one film will allow students to focus their analyses; the assignment is structured in such a way that students will have more luck with a mainstream film that has some nonwhite characters, rather than a movie that addresses the topic of race directly. If you want students to compare approaches, however, suggest that they examine films that are related—perhaps an original film and its remake, sequels, or a serious movie and one that satirizes it.

Successful papers will go beyond labeling a particular movie "racist" or "not racist." Stress to your students that they need to read the film closely, examining details they may not normally pay attention to. They should consider plot and characterization, of course, but they'll also need to assess how subtle cues inform the film's attitudes toward race. The questions listed in the assignment itself offer a useful heuristic for students unpracticed in film criticism. Encourage them to start their drafts by answering each one in turn, in as much detail as they can muster. Once they have some ideas down on paper, they'll be in a better position to craft a thoughtful response to the film or films they have viewed. Remind them that their final papers must take a position and support it with details, not simply answer individual questions.

Additional Resources

Nonfiction

Clint C. Wilson II and Felix Gutierrez, *Race, Multiculturalism, and the Media: From Mass to Class Communication* (1995) A second edition of Wilson and Gutierrez's *Minorities and the Media,* this book examines the relationships of America's four biggest racial groups as they are presented in the media. It also suggests how mass media is breaking apart as marketers continue to refine narrowing demographics.

Film

Bamboozled (2000) Spike Lee's consideration of race in Hollywood stars Damon Wayans as a TV writer who attempts to get fired by pitching a minstrel show, complete with blackface. To his surprise, the network executives love the idea.

Rebirth of a Nation (2004) Musician DJ Spooky remixed scenes from the original *Birth of a Nation* to bring out a "counter-narrative." Excerpts of the film and score and an essay on the project are available at http://www.djspooky.com/art.html.

Ira Glass, **Howard and Me** (p. 432)

Glass's praise for Howard Stern begs to be read in conjunction with David Nasaw's "The Pernicious 'Moving Picture' Abomination" (p. 411). Stern's show faces a censorship drive similar to what antivice crusaders launched against nickelodeons nearly a century ago. Both essays raise questions of how class considerations affect government regulation of popular entertainment. Students will more readily recognize how these issues inform "Howard and Me" if they have been exposed to David Nasaw's historical consideration of media censorship. The similarities between the two cases are striking.

Like nickelodeon movies, Howard Stern's radio show is most popular with a working class audience, and it is most reviled by educated listeners. Once students have examined issues of class and censorship in Nasaw's essay, ask them if they see similar dynamics affecting attitudes toward NPR and the *Howard Stern Show*. The former is clearly a highbrow venue; the latter is just as clearly low-brow. But as Glass points out, their content and structure are often quite similar; it's the context and the audience that underscore their difference. Ask your students why, then, Stern is so vulnerable to FCC oversight while programs like *This American Life* are practically ignored. Whose interests is the government protecting?

Interrogating Assumptions

Of the assumptions about entertainment explored in the chapter's introduction, the third is most relevant to Glass's argument. Critics and censors have gone after shows they consider indecent because, theoretically, their content poses a risk to children's innocence. Underpinning this logic is the idea that because children cannot be prevented from seeing or hearing publicly broadcast programs, we must protect them from the possibility of being exposed to anything that might harm them. If entertainment were truly a matter of personal choice, this risk would be of no concern. Note, too, that FCC enforcement is triggered by audience response. Rather than expect listeners and viewers to ignore programs they find offensive or inappropriate, the government officially encourages the public to respond by filing complaints.

Writing about Cultural Practices

This straightforward assignment calls for a research-based position paper on the topic of broadcast censorship. Although students may benefit from reading what others have written on this very contentious issue, the bulk of their research should be localized. That is, they should focus their investigations on how an area radio or television station has responded to the Federal Communications Commission's stricter indecency guidelines and more aggressive enforcement. In addition to tracking down a clear explanation of the FCC's rules (not an easy task, as Howard Stern himself has repeatedly pointed out on his program), students will need to obtain an official statement of policy from the broadcast outlet of their choice. This alone, however, will probably not be enough material from which to fashion a coherent argument. Suggest that your students, therefore, study multiple broadcast outlets in the area and investigate whether they

have been fined or threatened with a fine from the FCC and how they responded. In addition, interviews will be invaluable. If students cannot gain an
audience with representatives or employees of a station, encourage them to at
least talk with a few of the station's viewers or listeners regarding their perspectives on how (or if) the regulations have affected their favorite programs.

Additional Resources

Nonfiction

David Sedaris, *Me Talk Pretty One Day* (2000)   Sedaris's book of essays contains "Big Boy," the scatological piece to which Glass refers.

Film

Private Parts (1997)   Based on Stern's autobiography of the same name,
Private Parts presents the controversial figure as a likable nerd who takes on
the corporate powers that want to censor his show.

Web

Federal Communications Commission, http://www.fcc.gov/cgb/
consumerfacts/obscene.html   The FCC site's consumer facts section has
information on what constitutes obscenity, profanity, and indecency.

Kevin Arnovitz, **Virtual Dictionary** (p. 438)

Most fans of reality television understand that there is very little reality to it.
Viewers know, for example, that producers mine hundreds of hours of footage
to splice together a one-hour episode and that they use sophisticated editing
techniques to manufacture a program's story line. Your students may not, however, realize just how much manipulation goes into creating a reality television
series. Arnovitz's definitions include several revelations that will likely be new
for your students. Work with the class to compile a list of the details that surprise
them, and discuss how this new information affects their perceptions of so-
called unscripted television.

Some students may not have given much critical thought to the cultural
implications of the popularity of reality programs. You might want to show a 10-
or 15-minute segment from a current show as a reference point for discussion.
Then, using Arnovitz's definitions as cues, investigate with your class what the
various production strategies reveal about the purposes behind any given program. Why, for example, do so many shows film "testimonials," and why would
producers want to distort what participants say to the camera? What do shows
like *Big Brother* have in common with traditional game shows? With pornography? With tabloid journalism? As a final consideration, ask your students why

they think reality shows are as popular as they are. Now that the novelty has worn off, what makes people continue to watch these programs?

Writing about Cultural Practices

This assignment gives students the opportunity to extend the topic of class discussion to their own written analyses of a popular reality program. Students may be reluctant to unravel the threads of their favorite programs; to increase objectivity and critical awareness, encourage them to investigate a show that they haven't watched before. On one level, students will use information from Arnovitz's "Virtual Dictionary" to deconstruct several episodes of an unscripted show. In addition to applying his terminology to a focused example, student papers should attempt to answer the question posed in the assignment: What assumptions about the role or purpose of entertainment does this show rely on to keep people watching? Remind them that the chapter introduction offers some analysis of common assumptions that can serve as a starting point, but encourage them also to consider unrelated assumptions suggested by their observations. For added depth of analysis, suggest that they might question how assumptions regarding identity (see chapter 1), community (chapter 2), and romance (chapter 4) inform the program as well.

Additional Resources

Nonfiction

Annette Hill, *Reality TV: Audiences and Popular Factual Television* (2005)   Hill evaluates the appeal of reality television by questioning how its viewers understand the shows.

Film

The Truman Show (1998)   Jim Carrey plays a man unaware that his entire life is broadcast as a soap opera for viewers around the world.

Television

Colonial House   PBS has worked from the concept of reality television to create shows that immerse participants in a particular historical moment. *Colonial House* is one of a number of such programs, including *Frontier House* and *Manor House*.

Jennifer L. Pozner, **The Unreal World** (p. 442)

Of all the readings in this chapter, this cultural critique of reality TV offers the clearest explanation of why entertainment isn't just for fun (see assumption 1). Although "network execs . . . deny that the shows are meaningful in any other way" (par. 7), Pozner critically examines a multitude of examples to expose the cultural attitudes that both inform, and are reinforced by, one of the most popular entertainment vehicles of the early twenty-first century. She concludes that reality TV perpetuates negative stereotypes of women, men, and people of color.

Pozner crams a lot of analysis into a relatively short article. To keep students from becoming overwhelmed, you might want to work with your class to outline her points, making a list of her criticisms and the supporting evidence she offers for each. Although she focuses on relationship- and makeover-themed reality shows, her observations apply to most of the reality subgenres as well. Encourage your students to add their own support for (or against) her arguments, drawing on examples from shows that have been added to the mix since Pozner's piece was published in 2004.

The very name applied to unscripted television implies that "reality TV" is an objective and unfiltered representation of everyday life in the United States and, increasingly, in other countries. But as both Jennifer L. Pozner and Kevin Arnovitz (p. 438) reveal, the genre carefully manipulates raw footage to present a profoundly distorted reflection of contemporary culture. Worse, Pozner warns, the stereotypical images proffered by reality shows are as harmful to the people who see them as they are to the program's participants. In addition to asking why men and women are so willing to subject themselves to humiliation as contestants on these shows, ask your students why people watch them. Do they agree with Pozner's characterizations of these shows as sexist and racist?

Although Pozner makes several compelling points, some students may reasonably disagree with her conclusions, even using her own statements to undermine her argument. If, for example, viewers enjoy reality shows because they give the audience a sense of superiority over the people on the screen (par. 8), can that same audience be expected to accept stereotypes as unvarnished truth? Students who have read "The Pernicious 'Moving Picture' Abomination" (p. 411) and "Howard and Me" (p. 432) may notice as well that Pozner uses the same rationale for shunning these shows that antivice crusaders and Howard Stern opponents have used in their efforts to censor nickelodeon films and raunchy radio: They are harmful to children, who don't know enough to reject negative images of women or to question superficial portrayals of love as being built on physical beauty and money. In considering Pozner's analysis of the assumptions that inform reality TV, then, you might encourage your students to recognize and question the assumptions that inform her argument.

Writing about Cultural Practices

Writing a brief treatment of a new reality show idea gives students a chance to attempt something that Pozner does not: suggesting a solution to the problems she identifies. The challenge for students will be to imagine a reality show that will appeal to viewers without demeaning or humiliating its participants. This, in turn, requires students to think about what draws people to reality television and to question whether a friendly version of the genre could succeed. (They may want to check out other readers' responses to Pozner's article, and their questions about solutions, on the *Ms.* magazine website; see below for the URL.) If they conclude that their alternative would be doomed to failure by market forces, that's fine. They may write instead on why there can be no alternative to the genre as it now exists.

Additional Resources

Nonfiction

Sam Brenton and Reuben Cohen, *Shooting People: Adventures in Reality TV* (2003)   Tracing reality TV to roots in documentaries, soap operas, and shows like *COPS,* Brenton and Cohen conclude that the development of reality shows leads to psychological isolation for participants and viewers.

Television

Drawn Together   Comedy Central's animated parody uses stock characters and story lines to expose the artificiality of reality shows.

Web

Ms. magazine, http://www.msmagazine.com/arts/chat/2004-12-03-pozner.asp On the *Ms.* magazine website, readers chat with Jennifer L. Pozner about some of the issues raised in "The Unreal World."

Hemal Jhaveri, **Queer Eye: Searching for a Real Gay Man** (p. 449)

One thing people expect from mass entertainment is validation: We want to see ourselves reflected in the characters and personalities on the screen (see assumption 2). For those who aren't a part of the majority population, this can be a persistent source of frustration. Minority groups, if they are acknowledged by the entertainment media at all, often see themselves represented with negative or dismissive stereotypes. The genius of *Queer Eye for the Straight Guy* is that it embraces those stereotypes and transforms prejudice into a source of cultural validation.

Queer Eye is on the surface a simple makeover program that subverts the genre by focusing on men's appearances. But what drives the show is its humor. As Jhaveri notes, the "Fab Five" can be downright vicious with their witty comments about a participant's shortcomings. Many of their remarks, indeed, imply that the "straight guy" is a failure as a man, and it's significant that most guests agree to be made over either as a concession to an embarrassed girlfriend, fiancée, or wife, or as part of an effort to obtain one. The crux of the program, then, is the idea that gay men are better than straight men, a premise that the participants and the audience accept wholeheartedly. Without thoughtful application of humor, however, the show's underlying assumption would almost certainly have met with resistance, if not outright hostility, from the heterosexual community. For a careful examination of humor as a powerful tool of political and cultural critique, refer your students to Alain de Botton's essay "Comedy" (p. 390). For studies of the machinations behind reality television, see Kevin Arnovitz's "Virtual Dictionary" (p. 438) and Jennifer L. Pozner's "The Unreal World" (p. 442).

Not every observer is pleased by *Queer Eye*'s success. Several critics have argued that the show's enthusiastic embrace of stereotypes is harmful and degrading. Others, like Jhaveri, want to see "more complicated and varying depictions of gay men and women" on television. And several conservative groups would like to see gay characters removed from prime time entirely. Rather than debate whether or not mass media's representations of gay culture are realistic or fair, however, consider asking your students to examine the assumptions that inform each of these perspectives.

Writing about Cultural Practices

By asking students to consider media representations of the gay community in the context of representations of a visible minority group, this assignment should elicit a nuanced analysis of the impact of televised stereotypes on American consciousness. Each essay on the Media Awareness Network (MAN) website makes points that can be applied to gay stereotypes, and they should spark plenty of ideas for writers. Students will base their papers on two brief essays of their choice, but encourage them to work in their own observations of contemporary television as well. That is, as they draft their essays, students should find and analyze examples from their own television viewing.

Students will do best if they focus their analysis on a tightly narrowed topic. There are quite a few essays on the MAN website, some of them too general to serve as the foundation of a successful student paper. At the same time, students may find themselves overwhelmed by the number of topics they may choose from. Below is a list of the most promising short essays provided on the site. You might want to review it with your students and encourage them to identify the essay topic that most interests them before sending them off to the Web on their own.

Gays and Lesbians

"Representations of Gays and Lesbians on Television"

"Representations of Gays and Lesbians in Film"

"Gays and Lesbians in the News"

"Advertising and Gay Consumers"

Aboriginal People

"Common Portrayals of Aboriginal People"

"Aboriginal People in the News"

"Native Names and Imagery in Sports"

Girls and Women

"Beauty and Body Image in the Media"

"Sex and Relationships in the Media"

"Media Coverage of Women's and Men's Issues"

"Media and Girls"

"The Economics of Gender Stereotyping"

"Women Working in the Media"

Men and Masculinity

"Common Stereotypes of Men in Media"

"Children's Perceptions of Male Stereotypes"

Additional Resources

Television

Queer Eye for the Straight Girl   The sister show to *Queer Eye for the Straight Guy* does little to dispel stereotypes about homosexuals; while the formula of the original show might lead viewers to expect a team of stylish lesbians, they actually have only one female host, who is joined by several gay men.

Web

Queer Eye website, http://www.bravotv.com/Queer_Eye_for_the_Straight_Guy/ The *Queer Eye* site includes video clips from several episodes as well as the cast's "Hip Tips."

"Blind Leading the Bland," http://www.popmatters.com/tv/reviews/q/queer -eye-for-the-straight-guy.shtml   In this article from the online magazine *Popmatters*, Terry Sawyer compares the stereotyping of gays in *Queer Eye* to the pernicious tradition of minstrel shows.

Sarah Vowell, **Pop-A-Shot** (p. 454)

Vowell's piece offers a fitting conclusion to this chapter. Having read several essays that take issue with the media and critically examine the ways in which commercial entertainment influences culture, students may lose sight of the redeeming value of amusement as an emotional release. "Pop-A-Shot" the essay is a lot like Pop-A-Shot the game: It's fun, it's not overly taxing, and it provides balance.

"Pop-A-Shot" celebrates play, or engaging in a pointless activity. Although Vowell emphasizes throughout her essay that the game "has no . . . socially redeeming value whatsoever," she concludes with the observation that it has important personally redeeming value. Playing the game lets her take a break from the obligations and stresses of adulthood. It helps the player connect with friends, family, and childhood. And, Vowell implies, in doing something for pure enjoyment, she recharges herself, making her better able to tackle the challenges of daily life.

In fact, students may notice that tensions surface throughout Vowell's description of the game. Every paragraph includes not only a description of the sublime simplicity of Pop-A-Shot but also a reference to the complexities of real life: irritation, competition, failure, and embarrassment, among other things. You might want to discuss with your class how this rhetorical device complicates Vowell's meaning. Is the essay, in the end, a simple homage to a children's game, or is it a subtle reflection on the difficulties of adulthood? What, in Vowell's estimation, is the purpose of fun?

Writing about Cultural Practices

Vowell's assertion that goofing off is a civic duty plays on one of the most famous phrases of the Declaration of Independence: "life, liberty, and the pursuit of happiness." Although historians agree that "happiness," in the context of the declaration, refers to wealth and property, Vowell takes it literally: To be a true American, she argues, one must attempt to have fun. This assignment asks students to write a critical personal reflection modeled on Vowell's analysis of Pop-A-Shot. Like Vowell, students must identify a simple leisure activity that they're fond of and engage in on a regular basis. Their topic need not be a commercial game. Students might examine nearly anything that they enjoy but is unproductive: for example, reading trashy novels, playing solitaire, watching cartoons, window shopping, laying on the beach for hours, riding roller coasters, and so on.

Additional Resources

Nonfiction

Sarah Vowell, *Assassination Vacation* (2005) Vowell documents another favorite free-time activity: visiting the sites of famous assassinations. Her unusual travelogue is both funny and informative.

Music

Sheryl Crow, "All I Wanna Do"   In this song from *Tuesday Night Music Club,* Crow scorns the everyday world of work and responsibility for mindless pleasures and beer.

Web

The World Adult Kickball Association, http://www.worldkickball.com/ Kickball is one of several playground games enjoying a renewed popularity among adults. The World Adult Kickball Association has divisions across the country.

Mixing Words and Images:
Designing a Roadside Attraction (p. 459)

One of the most wonderful things about American roadside attractions is their often unintentional celebration of democratic principles. Most roadside wonders eschew elite ideals of aesthetics and high culture, dwelling instead on the personal, the quirky, and the accessible. Although Nasaw's essay focuses on commercial ventures, people with very little money and no formal training have created fantastic examples of the genre for their own edification, from American flags fashioned out of milk jugs filled with colored liquid to the now demolished but once glorious Palace Depression in Vineland, New Jersey (see weirdnj.com or watch *Eddie and the Cruisers*). With a little creativity and plenty of freedom to experiment, your students should be able to imagine a modest roadside attraction of their own. If they seem intimidated by the prospect, encourage them to keep the attraction personal and not to worry about its larger meanings until they've completed their brainstorming. Most will discover that after they've thought of something and put it aside for a day or two, they'll find cultural meanings they hadn't intended. Another excellent way to overcome any creative blocks is to start by imagining something that makes fun of local culture, as many popular roadside attractions were first intended to do.

In addition to visiting RoadsideAmerica.com, students may find inspiration for their projects in the photo books *Weird N.J.* and *Weird U.S.,* published by Barnes & Noble and available at most of the chain's stores. Started as a small self-published 'zine in New Jersey, the *Weird U.S.* franchise is growing exponentially and as of 2005 includes books on Texas, Pennsylvania, Florida, Wisconsin, and Illinois, as well as a television series on the History Channel. Students who are still stuck for ideas might try answering the questions posed in the text before they attempt to design an attraction. Often, thinking about what they want to express will help them find the best vehicle for expressing it.

As with all of the Mixing Words and Images assignments in *ReMix,* remind your students that the creative project is only part of their task. Once they have an image (however crude or sophisticated) of their roadside attraction in hand, students will write a paper that explains the thinking they put into it. In addition to elaborating on the details in their image and explaining what's entertaining about their attractions, successful student papers will consider what their projects suggest about the chapter introduction's three assumptions regarding entertainment. What does their attraction reveal about local culture? Does it reflect local attitudes, attempt to influence them, or a little of both? And finally, would residents of the area be able to avoid it, and if so, how (if at all) might it be expected to affect their consciousness?

Connecting to Culture: Suggestions for Writing (p. 460)

The writing assignments that conclude the chapter offer students an opportunity to synthesize the ideas they've encountered in the readings and to make some conclusions about the assumptions outlined in the chapter introduction.

From Production Codes to Ratings Systems: Hollywood and Censorship

Using David Nasaw's historical analysis as a starting point, this assignment calls for a research paper on a narrowly defined topic, the Motion Picture Association of America's (MPAA) rating system. To counter student tendencies to produce a report rather than a position paper, you might want to suggest that students examine the history of a single movie or look at one subcategory of the current MPAA guidelines, such as nudity, violence, drug use, and the like, and encourage them to ask questions about the ratings system as they research it. Why did the system emerge? What was the political context behind Jack Valenti's efforts? How has the voluntary system influenced the practice of filmmaking? How has it changed the economics of motion-picture production? Remind students that they need to produce a thesis and use their research to support it; asking questions will help lead them to an original argument.

Why This Does(n't) Matter: Making Your Case about Reality TV

This project asks students to write an academic essay modeled on three professional writers' cultural analyses. Their arguments should be founded on a close study of several episodes of one to three reality programs in the same subgenre—for example, extreme makeover, home improvement, or stranded-on-an-island shows. Students should craft a thoughtful critique of what they see rather than offer general opinions about the current popularity of unscripted television. Although students may refer to Arnovitz, Pozner, or Jhaveri as they develop their positions, most important is that they form an opinion based on their observations and defend their positions coherently.

Defining Modern American Humor

This project encourages students to test a compelling idea from the chapter by applying it to specific examples from popular culture. The assignment suggests that students look at two or three examples; you might opt to tighten their focus by requiring them to consider only one entertainment genre, such as stand-up comedy, television, cartoons, or film. They might further narrow their topics by choosing a subgenre, such as Latina comediennes, workplace situation comedies, prime-time animation, or popular films that satirize other movies. As they craft their analyses, students might want to research the background of a given comic, show, or movie, asking what the creator's intentions were and how the comedy was received by the public at large. They should also examine the political and social contexts surrounding the humor.

Interrogating Assumptions: Why Is(n't) This Entertaining?

This final assignment calls for a text-based comparative analysis that synthesizes ideas from the chapter by evaluating several individual readings. To ensure coherence, encourage students to select readings that are closely related thematically as well as in the way they address assumptions about entertainment. If you've assigned any of the Interrogating Assumptions or Connecting to Another Reading questions that follow some of the selections in the chapter, allow your students to use their responses as starting points for their drafts. A successful student essay will posit a thesis about one of the assumptions and use the readings to support it, rather than simply compare and contrast several selections.

6 Nature

. . . or, what's so natural about nature?

What *is* nature, anyway? As the chapter introduction acknowledges, this seemingly innocent question can be maddeningly difficult to answer. A review of simple definitions reveals that the word has several overlapping and conflicting denotations. Among other things, "nature" can refer to the forces that control the universe, to the outdoors, to an absence of human interference, to human and animal temperaments, and to biological characteristics. But it's the connotations that truly complicate the issue. Is nature superior to, or subject to, civilization? Is it a retreat or a threat? Is it a state to strive for or to overcome? At the same time, the idea of nature conjures the centuries-old dichotomy between the sacred and the profane. For many, the natural world is something to be protected and revered; for others, it's a resource to be manipulated for human benefit. The central questions, then, may be the most contentious: What is humanity's relationship with nature, and what should it be?

Bombarded by environmentalist messages, many students have come to resist them, and they may report that they don't enjoy what they perceive of as nature writing, even if they've never read any. It's probable that a contingent of your class will approach the study of this chapter with a certain amount of dread, worried that they'll be reading paeans to the glories of nature or prose lectures imploring them to recycle and respect the land. You'll be able to counter this fear by starting with one of the more iconoclastic essays in the mix: Susan Orlean's surreal "Lifelike" (p. 474) would be a good choice, as would Eric Schlosser's muckraking "Why McDonald's Fries Taste So Good" (p. 552). Once they've been reassured that the chapter is not what they might have expected, students will be in a better frame of mind to approach the more environmental essays; you may want to assure them that even those are not typical examples of nature or conservation writing. Before you have students read anything, you might consider exploring, as a class or through a preliminary journal assignment, what assumptions they currently hold about nature and the environment. Brainstorm as a group about what the word "nature" means to them and encourage students to express any misgivings they might have about studying it in a writing or cultural-studies class.

The Examining the Everyday assignment that opens the chapter will also go a long way toward dispelling student misconceptions. Rather than asking them about the environment, it compels them to think about consumer products and what marketing techniques reveal about cultural attitudes toward nature and what is deemed natural. Although the assignment prompts students to search magazines or the Internet for examples of products, you might suggest that they start their inquiries within their own living space. Most people will find at least one all-natural product sitting in one of their cabinets or on a shelf. Keep in mind that there are no incorrect answers to the questions posed in the text. The goal of the project is to get students thinking analytically and to question their own assumptions in a low-pressure context.

Because the central assumptions outlined in the chapter's introduction form the basis for analyzing the chapter's readings, spend some time discussing them in class. Use the questions that follow each discussion of an assumption to explore the concept with your students. You might want to ask your students whether they agree or disagree with the outlined assumptions, and what other assumptions about nature they can identify. Discuss with your class, also, how these assumptions function in American culture: Who holds them? What purposes do they serve? Are they helpful or harmful? And how do students see them played out in their personal lives and in the world around them?

All of the readings in this chapter question one or several of the three main assumptions outlined in the introduction—nature is a spiritual and nurturing force; nature is a person's essential character; and nature cannot be improved upon. Several featured scientists grapple with issues that these assumptions simplify. Naturalist Diane Ackerman offers a philosophical argument that attempts to redefine the relationship between humanity and nature, suggesting that they are too intertwined to imagine as separate entities. Psychologist Steven Pinker and biologist Susan McCarthy extend this notion to the theory of natural selection, respectively suggesting in "Against Nature" (p. 537) that genetics are impervious to human behavior and exploring in "On Immortality" (p. 544) how scientific research might overcome genetics after all. On a lighter side, journalists Susan Orlean and Eric Schlosser investigate the surprising practices of taxidermy and flavor chemistry to raise questions about how and why people manipulate nature, while Nobel Prize winner Wangari Maathai proposes that environmentalism might be the key to world peace. Four essays raise compelling questions about human nature and medicine: "American Bioscience Meets the American Dream" (p. 508) and "You—Only Better" (p. 517) explore the ethics of cosmetic and other elective surgeries, Jason D. Hill argues in "Save Lives! Defy Nature!" (p. 524) that biological instincts should not guarantee the right to bear children, and Lewis Thomas imagines a futuristic world in which society seeks to clone its best members. Turning to the world around us, creative nonfiction writers Barry Lopez and Annie Dillard explore landscape and wilderness to reveal how culture constructs unrealistic ideas about nature and to warn that romanticized notions can harm people as much as they do the environment.

With an abundance of science writing and complex philosophical questions, these readings are among some of the more conceptually challenging in *ReMix*. You'll likely want to save this chapter for later in the term, after students have gained some experience in critical analysis and are better prepared to approach challenging questions.

Additional Resources

Nonfiction

David W. Orr, *Earth in Mind: On Education, Environment, and the Human Prospect* (1994)   Orr suggests that modern education is misdirected, alienating students from the real business of living. He proposes new educational methods to reconnect people to the earth.

Henry David Thoreau, *Walden: Or, My Life in the Woods* (1862)   Thoreau, with his injunctions to "live deep," may be familiar enough that some students might be skeptical, but his fundamental work goes beyond nature to touch on politics, society, and the meaning of human existence.

Television

South Park, "Cherokee Hair Tampons"   In this episode, originally aired in 2000, Kyle needs a kidney transplant, but his parents and the townspeople reject modern medicine in favor of a holistic health store, from which they obsessively buy any product touted as all-natural.

Susan Orlean, **Lifelike** (p. 474)

In this cultural analysis, which was selected to be included in *Best American Essays* of 2004, Orlean points to a deep irony surrounding Americans' relationship with nature. The taxidermists she meets profess a love of animals—and they are sincere in their affection—yet their art depends on, and promotes, the ritual of trophy hunting. You may want to begin a class discussion of "Lifelike," then, by asking for students' general reactions. Based on Orlean's account, what are taxidermists trying to accomplish? How do your students respond to mounted animals when they see them? How does the setting—museum, theme restaurant, private home—affect their responses? Why?

The timing of taxidermy's popularity is significant. As Orlean reports, it established itself during the throes of the first Industrial Revolution, then reemerged during the environmental movement of the 1960s and '70s. In both periods, people struggled with the difficulties of urban living and questioned their relationship to nature. Victorians felt a desire to capture it; later activists felt compelled to rescue it. Taxidermy answers both of these needs, often with mixed results.

Central to taxidermy's philosophy is a desire to control wilderness, to impose a decidedly unnatural perfection on specimens from the natural world. The practice of stuffing and mounting dead animals is not an exercise in preserving nature, but rather an effort to improve upon it. Practitioners' emphasis on artistry, facial expressions, and composition, in particular, underscores the human desire to impose its own meanings on nature. Making dead animals look alive and putting them on display represents an attempt to deny human impact on the environment, even as resurrecting endangered and extinct species in imaginative displays is an attempt to overcome it. But as Orlean suggests, the closer taxidermists get to creating the illusion of life, the more surreal and discomfiting their art becomes. Ask your students what this suggests about the cultural consequences of manipulating nature.

Writing about Cultural Practices

Both of the writing assignments that accompany "Lifelike" ask students to analyze how cultural values are reflected in and influenced by animal displays and public simulations of the natural world. The first is a research project that requires students to draw on secondary interpretations of the Industrial Revolution in order to draw their own conclusions about the cultural meanings of modern taxidermy. The second assignment, based on field research and direct observation, encourages students to apply what they've learned about taxidermy to an original cultural analysis of simulated natural environments.

Additional Resources

Film

Psycho (1960)   In Hitchcock's classic horror movie, the creepy Norman Bates practices taxidermy, a hobby that seems to reflect his violent impulses.

Web

"The Horror of Everyday Life: Taxidermy, Aesthetics, and Consumption in Horror Movies," http://www.albany.edu/scj/jcjpc/vol2is4/horror.html Jeffrey Niesel examines taxidermy as a metaphor for psychopathy in *Silence of the Lambs* and *Texas Chainsaw Massacre II* as well as *Psycho*.

"A Shark in the Mind of One Contemplating Wilderness," http://www .thenation.com/doc/19991129/williams   Terry Tempest Williams's 1999 article for the *Nation* examines Damien Hirst's famously taxidermic art.

Barry Lopez, **The American Geographies** (p. 486)

This essay is surprisingly difficult, and it presents a complex argument that students might easily misread as exactly the type of romanticization that Lopez warns against. Explain to your class that few readers will fully grasp the point of "The American Geographies" in one reading. They should expect to read the essay at least twice, once for a gist of Lopez's central idea and the general direction his argument is taking and a second time to examine his claims and supporting points in depth. You might suggest that students draft a one- or two-sentence summary of each paragraph as they read, then use those sentences to construct a conceptual outline of Lopez's argument before they come to class to discuss it.

Just as Lopez reveals that the true American landscape contains many individual geographies, he structures his cultural critique around several discrete observations. The essay is organized into four sections, each of which makes a specific point. In the first part (pp. 486–88), Lopez establishes that although the United States comprises an "incomprehensible" number of sharply contrasting landscapes, the national reach of politics and media has conspired to construct an idealized generic national landscape that doesn't exist, and it has devalued intimate knowledge of local geographies in the process. He continues to an analysis (pp. 488–93) of how technological progress has divorced Americans from the land, warning that as people lose their sense of place, the natural environment becomes vulnerable to commodification and commercial exploitation. The third section of the essay (pp. 493–95) is an interlude of hope. Despite media pressures that gloss over the complexities of specific landscapes, Lopez observes that individual Americans continue to seek and nurture personal knowledge of their local environments. Those people, he insists in the next section, have a responsibility to share their knowledge with others, a practice he believes will eliminate the ignorance and carelessness that threaten to destroy the environment. Taken together, these mini-essays offer an overview of the challenges to American geography and culminate in Lopez's central claim that landscape and memory must both be preserved if a society is to survive.

Interrogating Assumptions

While Lopez acknowledges that nature can offer peace and serenity to those who seek it out, he draws a line between the romantic and the informed experience. To that end, Lopez emphasizes the authenticity of our experiences and finds that, unfortunately, in our culture most are deficient. He argues that a lack of intimate knowledge of American landscapes leads to crude generalizations and a collective ignorance. In turn, those who wish to exploit the land for commercial or political gain have only to manipulate a public that has few ties or genuine attachments to the land. What's left of the American wilderness has a small group willing to defend it. As Lopez writes, the only thing to do about our love of the land and our ignorance about it is to take the time to learn and respect it without romantic ideals.

Writing about Cultural Practices

This assignment asks students to share their intimate knowledge of a local geography in an effort to overcome the kind of ignorance that, according to Lopez, threatens the integrity of not only the land but also American society. Students may read Lopez's awed descriptions of American landscapes for inspiration, but stress to them that their passion for a particular region will be their most powerful muse. Remind your class of Lopez's point that outsiders know nothing of regions they haven't lived in. Students must describe a local geography well enough and in sufficient detail for a stranger to imagine it not only vividly but also accurately. You might remind them, as well, that geography is more than a collection of flora, fauna, waterways, and rock formations. Depending on their subject matter, students might add to their physical descriptions some limited discussion of local history, folklore, arts, and politics. In the spirit of Lopez's mission, be sure to distribute the final essays to everyone in the class, perhaps by asking students to bring enough copies to share, by emailing the files to class members, or by posting their papers on a course website.

Additional Resources

Fiction

Henry Beston, *The Outermost House: A Year of Life on the Great Beach of Cape Cod* (1928)   Though Beston meant to spend only a short time on Cape Cod, he became entranced by the particularities of the landscape and stayed throughout the year to observe the movements of animals and the changes of season.

Russell Mittermeier et al., *Wilderness: Earth's Last Wild Places* (2003)   A collaboration by several conservation groups, this book identifies remaining wilderness areas around the world and captures them in stunning photographs.

Web

Treehugger, http://www.treehugger.com/   This Internet filter points users to news about the environment and to ecologically sound products and practices.

Diane Ackerman, **We Are All a Part of Nature** (p. 498)

An accomplished poet and naturalist, Diane Ackerman rejects the popular dichotomy that distinguishes between nature and civilization. Human creations, she points out, are as much a part of nature as the weather is. Although people tend to think of nature as something outside of themselves, Ackerman reminds her readers that they cannot escape biology. No matter how much technology and culture humanity develops, in the end people are cellular organisms that will succumb to the same natural process that any other animal will. And regardless of how much we attempt to control those processes, we humans are susceptible to our animal essence: wildness, unpredictability, sex, hunger, violence. Ackerman takes the second assumption mentioned in the chapter introduction, that nature is a person's essential character, to its logical extreme: Nature *is* a person's nature.

Students may notice that despite her almost religious reverence for the natural world, Ackerman is a devoted scientist who firmly believes in the process of evolution. Some may object to her characterizations and counter her cultural analysis with the creationist stance that God made humans and that this makes humans superior to the natural world. Ackerman herself acknowledges that people disagree with her position. Encourage your students to comb Ackerman's essay for evidence that her view of evolution is not necessarily exclusive of creationism. They may find, for example, that her idea of "a powerful sense of belonging to the pervasive mystery of nature" is somewhat analogous to religious conceptions of God. Her main concern is that people not blithely assume that civilization excludes them from the laws of nature.

Interrogating Assumptions

Despite her glowing descriptions of the wonders of nature, Ackerman rejects romantic ideas that the environment is nurturing or renewing. She notes, instead, that nature is frequently hostile to life, violent, and uncontainable, and she emphasizes that human existence has its origins in "the flatulence of blue-green algae"—not a pretty thought. Her argument relies on a belief that maintaining a connection with nature is spiritual and healing, but she gives the notion a subversive twist by reminding her readers that their basest elements are a function of biology. We can't return to nature for renewal, she suggests, because we're already and unavoidably immersed in it.

Writing about Cultural Practices

Based on a close reading of a fairy tale or children's story, this assignment offers an interesting exercise in a cultural critique of an important artifact of childhood. Even inexperienced students should be able to fashion reasonable analyses from their own interpretations of a story and the discussion of cultural assumptions from the chapter's introduction. If you would like to encourage more complicated analyses, however, you might suggest that students add some secondary readings in psychological criticism or the social uses of fairy tales to their research. The works of Bruno Bettelheim, Clarissa Pinkola Estés, and Jan Harold Brunvand, in particular, will help to give them additional analytical handles for this project.

Additional Resources

Nonfiction

Diane Ackerman, *Cultivating Delight: A Natural History of My Garden* (2001)
    In the microcosm of her garden, Ackerman observes aspects of nature that serve as larger metaphors for life.

Desmond Morris, *The Naked Ape: A Zoologist's Study of the Human Animal* (1967)   Morris collapses the carefully held distinction between humans and other primates in this study, looking at mating, feeding, child rearing, and other habits to establish the link.

Web

The Talk.Origins Archive, http://www.talkorigins.org/   A Usenet group for the debate of evolution and creation, Talk.Origins archives old discussions online to "provide mainstream scientific responses to the many frequently asked questions that appear" in the newsgroup.

Wangari Maathai, **Trees for Democracy** (p. 501)

Wangari Maathai holds a profound respect for the natural environment. Your students might be surprised, therefore, to discover that the Nobel Prize–winning environmentalist does not advocate returning nature to its wild state or setting it aside to be preserved from further human development. Quite the contrary, Maathai argues that the land is a resource that must be managed for humanity's best interests. As she notes, nature offers "fuel, food, shelter, and income" (par. 13) to which everybody has a right. Problems arise not when individual citizens take advantage of their environment for personal benefit, but when powerful groups manipulate natural resources on a large scale without considering the immediate local effects and the long-term global implications of their actions. Rather than maintain a respectful distance from nature, Maathai suggests that responsible world citizens must take an active role as stewards of the environment. By doing so, she believes, impoverished peoples can not only reclaim the natural resources they need to survive but also stabilize weak governments, reinvigorate local cultures, and promote peace.

Students may need some help comprehending the interrelatedness of politics, culture, and environment that Maathai presents. As she envisions the current environmental and sociopolitical situation, nature has been devastated by capitalism, leaving the future of democracy hanging in the balance. You might want to work with your class to outline the processes Maathai describes. Unbridled commercial development commodifies the land and robs third-world peoples of the resources they need for survival. Forced by circumstances to join a profit-oriented system of selling and buying materials rather than producing and consuming only what they need, and disadvantaged by inequitable "international economic arrangements," local farmers are unable to compete in the marketplace. Left without resources or income, they succumb to poverty, which in turn breeds conflict, violence, and civic unrest. Speaking to a group of powerful world leaders and influential public figures, Maathai argues that the land belongs to all and that commercial interests should be discouraged, if not outrightly prevented, from exploiting natural resources for corporate profit at the expense of the general population. She does not, however, expect that this change will be effected by the leaders to whom she speaks. Rather, she asserts that it is the responsibility of local peoples to reclaim management of their environment, explaining that she has "always believed that solutions to most of our problems must come from us" (par. 6).

Students who have read this chapter's essays by Barry Lopez (p. 486) and Diane Ackerman (p. 498) might recognize that common themes run through all three works. Like Lopez, Maathai suggests that a commodified landscape threatens to undermine a society's political integrity and economic stability; she argues that individuals are best equipped to overcome the ravages of corporate behavior. And like Ackerman, she argues that humankind is inextricably linked with the natural world and cannot survive in isolation from the environment. Encourage your students to examine how Maathai expands upon these ideas and applies them to politics.

Interrogating Assumptions

Through the Green Belt Movement, Maathai combines science, social commitment, and active politics. This movement is a broad-based, grassroots organization whose central project is working with women's groups to plant trees to conserve their community's environment and improve the quality of their lives. Maathai has assisted women in planting more than 30 million trees to combat the loss of natural resources that leads to economic and political oppression, arguing that when communities are stripped of their resources, poverty, crime, and sickness ensue. As Maathai has stated, "Unless we properly manage resources like forests, water, land, minerals, and oil, we will not win the fight against poverty. And there will be no peace."

Writing about Cultural Practices

Service-oriented learning in the composition course is becoming increasingly popular, and this group assignment gives you and your students an opportunity to discover how working for community benefit can translate into personal growth and improved communication skills. To keep the project manageable, encourage your students to select a local issue that directly influences your campus or a disadvantaged population. Remind them, as well, that they are writing a proposal; they won't be expected to put their ideas into action.

Students should start by brainstorming a list of local problems, which don't necessarily have to be obviously environmental to be promising subjects for exploration. Once a group has selected an issue that interests them, they will need to research it: how it affects the local population, what solutions (if any) have already been proposed (by whom), and how those proposals have been received. They might interview local politicians, community activists, and students or local residents who are affected by a problem; some students may be interested in learning about the scientific principles behind the problem. Remind your students that in addition to identifying and understanding a problem, their primary task is to think of a possible solution for it. As they write their proposals, they should not only identify the problem and solution their group has settled on but also put some effort into mapping out the interconnectedness between an environmental problem, social issues, economic concerns, and politics. Students should be careful, as well, to identify the appropriate audience for their proposal and craft their proposals with the goal of convincing their readers to act on their ideas.

Additional Resources

Nonfiction

Sarah Erdman, *Nine Hills to Nambonkaha: Two Years in the Heart of an African Village* (2003)   A former volunteer and now an employee of the Peace Corps, Erdman tells the story of her tour doing community development in the Ivory Coast.

Web

Heifer International, http://www.heifer.org   Heifer International attempts to combat poverty by providing livestock to people in underdeveloped countries and teaching them sustainable animal husbandry.

Natural Resources Institute, http://www.nri.org/   The Natural Resources Institute researches sustainable development methods and educates people about them. Information on current projects is posted in their monthly newsletter.

Carl Elliott, **American Bioscience Meets the American Dream** (p. 508)

This essay and the essay by Christine Rosen that follows it explore the connections between medical technologies and self-fulfillment. Because they both consider social influences on identity construction, "American Bioscience Meets the American Dream" and "You—Only Better" (p. 517) may work well in conjunction with the questions of identity that inform the first chapter of *ReMix*.

In "American Bioscience Meets the American Dream," Carl Elliott looks at the popularity of medical "enhancement technologies"—cosmetic surgery and psychopharmacology in particular—to question the paradoxical idea that the best way to nurture one's emotional self is to manipulate one's physical self. He notes that, while Americans tend to believe that identity is fixed by nature (see assumption 2 in the chapter introduction), the culture also believes that nature prevents people from fulfilling their true selves (see assumption 3). Elliott attempts to resolve this contradiction by suggesting that social pressures, not nature, define Americans' sense of what the ideal self is and can be.

The essay explores several specific case studies to reveal the complex ways in which social ideals—Elliott calls them "stigmas"—pressure individuals to conform to external expectations at any cost. In each case, a specific challenge of living in the modern world (such as violence or obsession with celebrity) leads a person to transform him- or herself physically in order to cope. However, Elliott notes that for each person he describes this physical transformation is conceived as the path to self-fulfillment, not an admission of failure. Students likely will have varying opinions regarding each of the enhancement technologies Elliott cites. These degrees of acceptability are part of the phenomenon the author explores: Why does American culture accept the use of antidepressants, for example, but remain horrified by voluntary amputations? If some enhancements are more tolerable than others, what social factors might be contributing to their acceptability? Elliott explains that the complex interrelationships between ever-changing social norms and pharmaceutical advances result in new conceptions of illness with every generation. Once a physical or psychological reality *can* be changed, that condition is redefined as a pathology, which in turn provides a moral justification for seeking medical solutions to what are, at core, social problems.

Writing about Cultural Practices

The basic principle of modern advertising is to create an insecurity, then offer a product that promises to relieve it. Couple that dynamic with the powerful stigmas that enhancement technologies claim to treat and consumers are hard-pressed to evade the social and psychological effects. Students' challenge for this assignment is to examine several medical-solution ads carefully and apply Elliott's insights to an analysis of how they manipulate self-image to sell a product or procedure.

In addition to analyzing the text (written or verbal) and imagery of several advertisements, students should evaluate how context contributes to the ads' effects. With television spots, for example, students might consider the programming they interrupt. If they are looking at a print ad, they might consider the topic, approach, and intended audience. In the case of the Web, they might compare destination sites and pop-up ads. Some students may want to examine how messages promoting the same product vary according to the medium and context in which they appear.

You may want to explain to your students that evaluating audiences can be tricky when it comes to surgical and prescription products. Although ads may be targeted directly at consumers, potential customers must persuade a medical professional, as well as an insurance carrier, to provide the service or product. A person convinced by a commercial for Prozac, for example, can't simply walk into the nearest drugstore and buy a month's supply off the shelf. Ask your students to consider why, then, television spots and magazine ads for the antidepressant are so ubiquitous. Do marketers truly expect consumers to call their doctors, as most of the ads urge them to do? Or is the aggressive marketing of closely regulated products and procedures meant to influence cultural attitudes in general?

Additional Resources

Nonfiction

W. E. B. DuBois, *The Souls of Black Folk* (1903)   DuBois's landmark book of essays describes a feeling of double consciousness that characterizes the lives of some African Americans, who see themselves both through the lens of their experiences and through the perception of how white America views them.

Elizabeth Haiken, *Venus Envy: A History of Cosmetic Surgery* (1997)   Haiken examines the tensions between medical necessity and consumer demand that have shaped the cosmetic-surgery industry.

Charles Taylor, *The Ethics of Authenticity* (2005)   Even as aspects of modern life become more artificial, the idea of authenticity has taken on a moral force. Taylor explores why realness is so important to our society and how our distaste for falsity may be an asset.

Film

The Stepford Wives (2004)   This remake of the 1975 movie stars Nicole Kidman as a newcomer to the town of Stepford, where all of the wives are uncannily perfect.

Web

Paxil, http://www.paxil.com   The consumer-oriented website for Paxil, an antianxiety medication, includes tests that encourage people to self-diagnose.

Christine Rosen, **You—Only Better** (p. 517)

In this excerpt from "The Democratization of Beauty," Christine Rosen explores the cultural consequences of the dynamics explained by Carl Elliott in "American Bioscience Meets the American Dream" (p. 508). Although social pressures may drive individuals' desires to modify their bodies for self-fulfillment, as Elliott suggests, Rosen points out that when enough people choose to make such modifications, the surgically enhanced population exerts an equally insidious pressure on society. The result is an endless cycle of raised standards, lowered self-esteem, and increasingly extreme solutions.

Cosmetic surgery is a prime example of human efforts to improve on nature (see assumption 3 in the chapter introduction). Rosen argues that although medical procedures offer temporary external improvements for individual people, and although they may indeed make some patients truly happy, they do so at the expense of personal and social well-being. By enabling cultural denial of the physical limits imposed by nature, Rosen believes, cosmetic surgery encourages a general overemphasis on physical appearance, diminishes the more socially valuable qualities an individual might strive for, and weakens the nation's character. Although popular rhetoric suggests that cosmetic enhancement is a democratic tool for leveling the social playing field, Rosen warns that the opposite is true. Rather than question unattainable standards of beauty, we have instead made them surgically attainable, doubly handicapping those who choose to accept what they "would naturally look like without constant nipping, tucking, peeling, and liposuctioning" (par. 7) and reinforcing social inequalities based on appearance.

If students question the validity of Rosen's assertion that Americans have come to view cosmetic surgery as something anybody can obtain, consider sharing this passage from another part of "The Democratization of Beauty":

> In a mere decade (between 1982 and 1992), according to the American Academy of Cosmetic Surgery, the number of people surveyed who said they approved of cosmetic surgery increased by 50 percent, and the number who disapproved declined by 66 percent. Consumer demand for surgery has skyrocketed alongside the evaporation of this disapproval. As Alex Kuczynski wrote recently in the *New York Times*, "The American Society of Aesthetic Plastic Surgery reports that the overall number of cosmetic procedures has increased 228 percent since 1997. The numbers are likely to rise as the population ages, prices drop, younger patients seek out surgery, technology and genetic engineering generate new techniques, and more doctors from various fields offer cosmetic surgical procedures."

Writing about Cultural Practices

As students research and write about this challenging topic, encourage them to consider both Elliott's insights regarding the uses of enhancement technologies for self-fulfillment and Rosen's warnings about the social consequences of widespread cosmetic surgery. You might suggest that they start by rereading the paragraphs of "American Bioscience Meets the American Dream" in which Elliott briefly addresses the issue. The tensions between these two perspectives are at the heart of current debates over ethnic minority women and men who undergo the knife in a quest for a more Caucasian appearance. While patients often insist that the surgery improves their position in a white-dominated society and gives them personal advantages, or that it simply makes them feel better about themselves, they are often accused of betraying their race or displaying self-hatred. A central question students will need to consider, then, is what the relationship is between individual desires and responsibility to a community. Note, too, that it will be helpful if students have already studied the chapters on community and tradition.

Additional Resources

Nonfiction

Sander L. Gilman, *Creating Beauty to Cure the Soul: Race and Psychology in the Shaping of Aesthetic Surgery* (1998)   Analyzing how cosmetic surgery has been used to combat psychological ailments, Gilman traces how physiognomy has at times fed into racism.

Television

Nip/Tuck   The FX series follows the lives of two plastic surgeons: One is an Adonis obsessed with his own image while the other is susceptible to misgivings about the value (or harm) of his work.

Starved   This FX series, a comedy about a support group for people with eating disorders, has aroused anger among some groups for making light of a serious problem.

Web

"Changing Faces," http://www.time.com/time/asia/covers/1101020805/ story2.html   This report, by *Time Asia*'s Lisa Takeuchi Cullen, explores the rising popularity of cosmetic surgery and speaks to the controversial practice among Asian women of having surgery to look more European.

Jason D. Hill, **Save Lives! Defy Nature!** (p. 524)
Four Letters Responding to "Save Lives! Defy Nature!" (p. 528)

Although Jason D. Hill makes some serious points about an important issue, students may be put off by the hostility and name calling that pervades "Save Lives! Defy Nature!" Any negative or defensive reactions offer an excellent opportunity to discuss how tone affects audience response to a writer's argument. Ask students if Hill's article would be more or less effective if he had taken a calmer or more respectful approach. What does he accomplish by deliberately angering his audience?

At heart, Hill takes issue with the assumption that the instinctive drive to procreate guarantees a person's right to have children, and he emphatically rejects the idea that natural human characteristics should always be nurtured. Putting questions of biological imperative aside, Hill reminds his readers that childbearing has social consequences. Because a person's decision to have children affects both those children and the people in their communities, Hill argues that society has an obligation to ensure that only qualified adults become parents. It's important to note that Hill does not suggest how society might meet this obligation. Proposing a solution is not his purpose. Instead, his goal with this article is to shock his readers into awareness of a problem. He wants to prompt "a national debate on the so-called right to reproduce" (par. 5). By making people angry, Hill forces them to give the issue their attention. His points may be divisive, but he makes them hard to ignore.

Hill's concerns are hardly new. For decades, the Chinese government has successfully used financial incentives to discourage its citizens from bearing more than one child per family. Since at least the 1960s, environmentalists have been advocating zero population growth, warning that rising birthrates around the globe are overburdening the planet's resources. At least for now, American politicians and commentators have avoided the issue, largely because any suggestion of "governmental intrusion into the reproductive lives of human beings" (par. 5) tends to invoke extremely negative reactions. Although the nation may have let the issue slide despite Hill's hopes, encourage your students to take up the debate in class. Should society consider limiting reproductive rights? Pointing them to readers' letters to *Salon* about Hill's article, you might ask your students why people feel so strongly about the right to have children. They may also consider whether the burden of child rearing should be placed on individual parents, as Hill assumes, or on the community as a whole. (For a different perspective on the links between biological urges and society, refer students to Steven Pinker's essay "Against Nature" on p. 537.) What other factors might contribute to the contemporary problem of pathologically neglected children? Are there potential solutions that don't involve restricting individuals' rights to pro-create?

Finally, you might ask your students to question how serious Hill really is. Although he starts with the suggestion that society limit people's reproductive rights, he makes several observations about the shortcomings of society and parents that imply he doesn't truly believe this. Like Jonathan Swift before him, could Hill be sarcastically proposing an absurd solution in order to force his readers to contemplate more realistic options?

Writing about Cultural Practices

For this assignment, students will examine the techniques used by two writers to address a serious issue. They might be able to make some headway by relying on the excerpt of Swift's famous manifesto reprinted on page 526, but they'll do better to read a complete version of "A Modest Proposal," easily found online (see the links that follow this entry) or in the library. In addition to reading each argument closely, students might enhance their analyses if they do some general research into the social and political contexts surrounding both Swift's and Hill's proposals. They may also incorporate published contemporary responses to both arguments into their papers.

Additional Resources

Web

The Population Connection, http://www.populationconnection.org/ This advocacy group, formerly known as Zero Population Growth, educates people about stabilizing population growth so as not to tax the earth's natural resources.

Letters on Salon.com, http://archive.salon.com/mwt/letters/2001/07/13/letters_breeding/index1.html Hill's essay inspired some heated responses, some of which you can read at Salon.com.

Jonathan Swift, "A Modest Proposal," http://darkwing.uoregon.edu/~rbear/modest.html This Web version of Swift's essay, hosted by the University of Oregon, may provide a useful comparison for students.

Lewis Thomas, On Cloning a Human Being (p. 532)

In the three decades since Thomas wrote this famous essay, human cloning has moved from the realm of science fiction to the center of an ethical and political storm. The debate surrounding cloning has shifted drastically since Lewis

Thomas first warned against attempting to duplicate socially valuable individuals. His wonderfully absurd scenario effectively proved that vanity cloning will always be impossible, regardless of what technological advances scientists might produce. Most contemporary commentators worry that human clones will be used as involuntary organ and tissue donors or as tools for genetic engineering. Scientific interest in cloning in the early twenty-first century focuses on harvesting stem cells from embryonic tissue to cure disease. Moral objections generally focus on the question of whether stem cells represent viable human beings. Few people continue to harbor Thomas's concern that cloning will be used to reproduce specific people in a perverse quest for immortality.

Although the focus of the issue may have changed, this essay's insights into the nature of individuality are invaluable. Using fantastical notions of human cloning to ground his argument, what Thomas really explores is the question of whether people are defined by their biological characteristics or by social influences. He offers a unique twist on the enduring "nature-versus-nurture" debate, siding squarely with those who theorize that social factors are more significant to a person's psychological development than biology is. "Nature" itself, Thomas argues, is not a matter of cells, tissue, and DNA, but the sum total of the complex interconnections of all of the people in an individual's life. Each of those people contributes to a person's identity—whether that influence is major or minor, recognized or not. Change just one of those elements, says Thomas, and what we think of as a person's nature will be profoundly altered. If this is the case, you might ask your students what becomes of the notion (see assumption 2) that people's most ingrained personality traits are simply their "nature."

Writing about Cultural Practices

Be aware that debates surrounding stem-cell research and "therapeutic cloning" are contentious and very heated at times. As students begin their research, stress to them that they need not choose a position on the issue. Rather, their task is to familiarize themselves with the current state of cloning technology, to discover what prominent scientists have identified as the key issues, and to share their findings with the rest of the class. To keep them focused, they should consider only the formal writings of respected scientists and bioethicists and stay away from broadcast interviews, blogs, and popular magazines.

Additional Resources

Nonfiction

Francis Fukuyama, *Our Posthuman Future: Consequences of the Biotechnology Revolution* (2002)   Fukuyama argues that advances in biotechnology will entail changes to the nature of human existence as drastic as those that followed the invention of language.

Film

Austin Powers: The Spy Who Shagged Me (1999)   Students will likely be familiar with this reference to human cloning: The villain in *Austin Powers*, Dr. Evil, produces a smaller version of himself, Mini-Me.

Multiplicity (1996)   Michael Keaton stars as an overextended man who clones himself in order to relieve some of his home and work duties, but the division of labor soon starts to bring out different sides of his personality.

Web

Duke Institute for Genome Sciences and Policy, http://www.genome.duke.edu/ This multidisciplinary organization is dedicated to addressing both the medical and social consequences of genome science.

Steven Pinker, **Against Nature** (p. 537)

For students without a background in biology, genetics, or Darwinian theory, Pinker's argument may produce some frustration. It may help to inform them that Pinker's essay attacking the tenets of sociobiology is part of an ongoing and often hostile debate with Stephen Jay Gould. Gould has attacked the central idea of evolutionary psychology—that genetic imperative alone explains evolution—as ridiculously oversimplified. In many ways, these competing scientific camps, both of which are grounded in Darwin's theories of natural selection, are asking which came first, the chicken or the egg (a riddle that Pinker alludes to in par. 7). If your students are struggling with the essay, however, assure them that they don't need to fully understand the science behind the debate in order to appreciate the underlying point that scientists have yet to satisfactorily explain the links between human biology and human behavior.

Spend some time with your students teasing out both the argument that Pinker makes and the argument he is responding to. It may be useful to create an outline of each argument and its supporting evidence on the board. Essentially, Pinker rejects the basic premise of sociobiology, which posits that human behavior is designed to propagate the species. He aims to supplant this theory with evolutionary psychology, which counters that genetic copying propagates human behaviors. He offers anecdotal evidence to support or undermine each position, concluding that evolutionary psychology is the more logical of the two. Individual humans may exhibit nonadaptive behaviors, he explains, but our genetic programming ensures that enough humans will procreate to continue generating copies of adaptive genes.

If you'd rather avoid re-creating the debate in class, approach Pinker's essay from the perspective of *ReMix*'s assumptions. How, you might ask your students, does Pinker's argument counter cultural assumptions that nature is a positive and nurturing force, that a person's essential characteristics are simply his or her nature, or that nature can't be improved upon? How do competing theories of evolution complicate these ideas?

Writing about Cultural Practices

Students need not understand a word of Pinker's essay to successfully complete this exercise, as the brief explanation of adaptive biology offered in the assignment should be sufficient to ground their explorations. By asking them to consider how adaptation works in a familiar social setting, in fact, this writing project may help them to better grasp the evolutionary questions that Pinker raises.

Additional Resources

Nonfiction

Charles Darwin, *The Origin of Species* (1890)   Darwin's book constitutes the foundation of evolutionary science. While other scientists claimed to have proposed the theory first, Darwin lined up the evidence from his observation of species to back up the idea.

Stephen Jay Gould, *The Structure of Evolutionary Theory* (2002)   In a book that took years to complete, Gould attempts to revise the basic tenets of Darwinism, which he believes have become so rigid as to be a hindrance to further discovery.

Film

Evolution Boxed Set (2001)   This eight-hour series from PBS begins with a film called *Darwin's Dangerous Idea,* in which dramatizations of key moments in Darwin's life are interspersed with comments by current evolutionary experts.

Other Essays in ReMix

Benedict Carey, "The Brain in Love" (p. 341)

Lewis Thomas, "On Cloning a Human Being" (p. 532)

Susan McCarthy, **On Immortality** (p. 544)

The introduction to chapter 6 asks the question, "If we have the ability to improve or prolong someone's 'natural' life through medicine, shouldn't we do so?" Susan McCarthy's answer is a resounding "No!" As Lewis Thomas does in his essay on cloning (see "On Cloning a Human Being," p. 532), McCarthy uses absurd scenarios and a good dose of humor to suggest that, although human immortality may someday be technically possible, its practical consequences effectively render it unlikely to ever actually happen.

This essay devotes a significant amount of attention to scientific research that promises to increase human longevity or, at the very least, to improve people's health in the final years of their lives. Raising serious questions about genome researchers' intentions, McCarthy warns that if we manage to find a way to increase life span while simultaneously slowing the aging process, humans may find themselves facing the possibility of immortality but lacking the moral sophistication to know what to do with it. Regardless of how realistic the possibility may be, however, McCarthy is more interested in exploring the ethical and social issues raised by rapid medical advances. Work with your students to compile a list of these issues, asking which are most serious and whether McCarthy's concerns can be resolved.

Because McCarthy also spends a good amount of time examining how natural selection may inevitably interfere with longevity, consider teaching "On Immortality" in conjunction with "Against Nature." Ask your students how Steven Pinker's observations about selfish genes and human behavior might inform McCarthy's analysis of human evolution in a world populated with immortals. Would he agree with her assertions or not?

Interrogating Assumptions

McCarthy suggests that, although science may consistently find ways to improve upon nature, many technological advances can have unintended negative consequences. At the same time, Mother Nature has an uncanny way of thwarting whatever advances might develop. Every improvement brings with it some kind of trade-off, whether biological or social, and McCarthy wants her readers to consider seriously what the personal, social, and political drawbacks of longevity and immortality might be.

Encourage your students to unearth some of the unexamined assumptions that inform McCarthy's argument. She implies, for example, that genome researchers are actively looking to make immortality a possibility. She also assumes that most people do indeed want to live as long as possible (as long as they can be "dewy fresh"). But is this true? What other impulses and cultural goals might be driving genome research and cultural support for it? What, besides longer life, might these experiments be after?

Writing about Cultural Practices

This assignment calls for a critical analysis of how themes of aging or immortality are presented in a science-fiction film. You may want to screen a movie and require that the entire class write about it, or you might opt to give them more choice (see below for some film suggestions). Be willing to move beyond the sci-fi genre if there's a particular film that intrigues you or your students. Anything that addresses questions of immortality or enduring youth, whether technically a comedy, drama, or children's story, is in some respects science fiction as well. Because the assignment focuses on sci-fi, the film(s) students watch will likely offer a cautionary tale that underscores the ironic aspects of endless youth or immortality. Warn students that summarizing a movie's plot or paraphrasing its moral is not a sufficient response to the assignment. Successful student papers will craft an argument about the film's intent and its message; they will also consider how assumptions about nature are reflected or refuted in the story and make some effort to compare the theme of the film to the themes of either Susan McCarthy's "On Immortality" or Lewis Thomas's "On Cloning a Human Being" (p. 532).

Some possible movie choices include:

AI	*Highlander*
Blade Runner	*Interview with the Vampire*
City of Angels	*The Island*
Cocoon	*The Picture of Dorian Gray*
Death Becomes Her	*Pirates of the Caribbean*
Dr. Heidegger's Experiment	*Tuck Everlasting*
Freejack	*Wings of Desire*
Gattica	

Additional Resources

Nonfiction

Steven Austad, *Why We Age: What Science Is Discovering about the Body's Journey through Life* (1997)   Austad presents theories of both how we age on a cellular level and why it is necessary for humans to age.

Stephen G. Post and Robert H. Binstock, *The Fountain of Youth: Cultural, Scientific, and Ethical Perspectives on a Biomedical Goal* (2004)   This book reviews the historical search for longevity, current ideas about antiaging, and social attitudes toward immortality.

Web

Immortality Institute, http://imminst.org/   The Immortality Institute views death as a disease that we should work to cure.

National Institute on Aging, http://www.nia.nih.gov/   This subdivision of the National Institutes of Health researches the aging process and provides health information.

Eric Schlosser, **Why McDonald's Fries Taste So Good** (p. 552)

As the chapter-opening assignment notes, American consumers put a great deal of confidence in natural products, assuming that something labeled "natural" is healthy, pure, and superior to manufactured consumables. But as Schlosser reports, the "natural flavor" used to enhance one of the country's most popular foods, as well as nearly all of the processed foods found in grocery stores and fast-food chains, is actually derived from a mind-boggling mix of chemicals. What's more, government regulations have created a bizarre situation in which the flavor compounds that can be called natural are often more processed, and less healthy, than artificial flavorings are.

Schlosser's background in journalism shows in his tone. Despite the shocking revelations that pervade his essay, he maintains an objective stance and refrains from offering his opinions about the flavor industry. In addition to asking your students to consider how this rhetorical device influences the effectiveness of Schlosser's writing, encourage them to explore the implications of his findings. Ask students to keep in mind the cultural assumption that nature can't be improved upon (see p. 471), and the assumption implied in the opening assignment, that natural products are superior. Begin by asking whether the widespread practice of using chemical flavor additives is a problem. Schlosser is careful to acknowledge, for example, that the taste of a freshly picked strawberry comes from chemical substances found in the fruit. So does it matter if scientists replicate that flavor with an elaborate combination of extracted chemicals? Why do "flavorists" and manufacturers keep the trade's practices secret? Remind students, as well, to consider not only the drawbacks of processed foods but also their benefits. With careful thought, some might conclude that the advantages of mass-produced food outweigh cultural distaste for how it is made.

Interrogating Assumptions

Changes to the ingredients and tastes of food occurred in concert with the rise of processed foods. As manufactured foods first emerged in the mid-nineteenth century, as nationally branded baked goods displaced corner bakeries in the early twentieth century, and again as mass-produced snack foods and TV dinners became commonplace in the 1950s, manufacturers sought ways to ensure that consumers would find their products tasty. Since the methods used to create processed foods tend to strip them of their flavor, producers turned to chemical companies for flavor additives. Not surprisingly, as realistic synthesized flavors became more attainable and more commonplace, they became more accepted by consumers, most of whom are unaware of what's actually in the food they buy. Schlosser doesn't comment directly on the idea that nature can't be improved upon, but throughout the essay he strongly implies that synthesized flavors are frequently more palatable than natural flavors.

Writing about Cultural Practices

Students' first inclination for this assignment might be to investigate junk foods, but remind them that nearly everything that can be found in a grocery store is processed. Canned peas, organic salad dressings, veggie burgers, whole-grain bread, and bottled spices are as affected by the work of flavorists as Twinkies and Lunchables are. Ingredient lists for fast-food products can usually be found on a poster or booklet in the restaurant or at the company's website. Although the assignment allows students to examine a food that someone else eats, strongly encourage them to focus on their own favorites. The shock of their discoveries will likely prompt them to think critically about how their own eating habits are influenced by cultural practices and assumptions.

You might want to require that students research any ingredients they don't recognize or can't define. If they discover, for example, that their favorite rolls contain "azodicarbonamide," make sure that they also discover that azodicarbonamide is a chemical that stabilizes leavened dough; in other words, it prevents yeast from expanding out of control. In many cases, students will not be able to find any information on an ingredient. When that happens, suggest they consider why the information is unavailable.

Finally, remind students that they are expected to do more than prepare a report on what ingredients are in their favorite foods. The purpose of the assignment is to get students thinking about how cultural attitudes and industry practices affect their diets and to take a clear position on the question of whether or not food labels provide enough information for consumers to make informed choices.

Additional Resources

Fiction

Patrick Suskind, *Perfume: The Story of a Murderer* (2001)   In Suskind's novel, an eighteenth-century Parisian perfume apprentice, born with a highly developed sense of smell but no smell of his own, starts killing women in search of the perfect scent ingredient.

Film

Supersize Me (2004)   Filmmaker Morgan Spurlock lives on a diet of only McDonald's food for 30 days. Through the course of his experiment, he gains weight, has an increase in cholesterol, and experiences symptoms of addiction.

Web

Slow Food USA, http://www.slowfoodusa.org/   The Slow Food movement began as a backlash to processed fast foods. Its proponents advocate local ingredients, heterogeneous food traditions, and general mindfulness about consumption.

Annie Dillard, **Living Like Weasels** (p. 565)

Annie Dillard's essay brings this chapter full circle. While "Nature" started with Susan Orlean's study of human attempts to perfect animals, it concludes with Dillard's assertion that animals hold the key to perfecting human beings.

Not a typical piece of nature writing by any means, "Living Like Weasels" will reward a close reading. Spend some time with your students examining Dillard's language and imagery: Although they may have come away from a first reading with the impression that Dillard romanticizes the natural world, they might quickly discover that she not only evokes the hostility, violence, and danger of wilderness, but she also underscores how closely intertwined the natural environment and human civilization already are. Consider, for example, the way Dillard describes Hollins Pond in the fourth paragraph of the essay: Not only is it essentially a swamp (six inches deep and overrun with lily pads), but litter and other evidence of human contact are as prevalent as the plants and animals; the fields and woods are framed by a highway and a "nesting pair of wood ducks." Even the name of her spiritual muse, "weasel," has strongly negative and anthropomorphic connotations. Nature, for Dillard, is not an escape from civilization, regardless of how much people (herself included) would like to think of it that way. Instead, it is a reminder of what civilized living can be.

It may take some effort to convince students that Dillard is not suggesting that people should live literally as weasels do. Rather, what she admires about weasels is their uncompromising willingness to live as nature intended them to. These animals do not question who they are, decide what they want to be, or try to improve themselves; they just are. What Dillard hopes to achieve in her own life is a comparable purity of mind, an unyielding devotion to a single purpose in life, whatever that purpose might be.

Interrogating Assumptions

In several ways, Dillard's musings rely on two of the assumptions about nature outlined in the chapter's introduction. Many passages in "Living Like Weasels" portray nature as a spiritual and nurturing force, and her central claim is that a person's essential characteristics *are* her nature. The wild, as she imagines it, is purer and more authentic than modern humanity is. Dillard does not, however, accept these assumptions entirely. She subverts them both to some degree, suggesting on the one hand that the purity of nature is inseparable from its inherent violence and destructive powers and arguing, on the other, that the problem with society is that people are unwilling to embrace their true natures.

Writing about Cultural Practices

The method outlined by this assignment should be an effective way to prompt student creativity and ground a critical analysis of a personal encounter.

Encourage them to mimic the structure of Dillard's essay—objective facts, personal observation, interpretation—if it helps them to organize their ideas, but allow students to follow whatever approach works best for them.

Additional Resources

Nonfiction

Annie Dillard, *Pilgrim at Tinker Creek* (1974)   Dillard's Pulitzer Prize–winning essay collection is rooted in minute attention to nature. No pure romantic, Dillard relates what is frightening in her surroundings as well as what is beautiful.

Film

Contact (1997)   Jodie Foster plays a scientist on a quest to discover the spiritual significance of human existence. She believes that other forms of intelligent life will provide a key to understanding humans.

Web

Anthropomorphism.org, http://anthropomorphism.org/   While many scientists dismiss anthropomorphism as a faulty way of thinking, researchers at Carnegie Mellon explore how it shapes our experience of the world and how it may influence future technologies.

Mixing Words and Images: Picturing Nature (p. 571)

Before they get started on this project, students would do well to reread Barry Lopez's "The American Geographies" (p. 486), which explains how idealized images of the environment promote political, economic, and cultural interests, and Annie Dillard's "Living Like Weasels" (p. 565), which reminds readers that nature can be as vicious as it is inspiring.

Identifying an idealized image of nature and designing a calendar, poster, or cartoon that works against it will likely be fun for your students. Keep in mind, however, that their purpose is to make a specific argument about nature and the assumptions that surround it. To this end, you might want to encourage them to draft their analyses before they design their artwork. At the very least, students should make some attempt to answer the questions on page 571 before they start crafting the visual element of the project. Students' efforts will be more productive if they locate in advance an idealized image they can respond to, determine who their audience will be, decide what they want that audience to take away from their images, and articulate the assumptions they hope to debunk.

To help your students plan their projects, you might want to evaluate as a group some well-known images that directly question idealized concepts of nature. Some possible examples include the gritty and ironic landscape images produced by the Farm Security Administration's photographers (especially those by Dorothea Lange, Arthur Rothstein, Russell Lee, and Marion Post Wolcott) during the Depression, the gruesome antivivisection posters distributed by People for the Ethical Treatment of Animals (PETA), the infamous ducks coated in oil in the wake of the *Exxon Valdez* disaster, or the documentary photographs collected by the Environmental Protection Agency in the late 1960s and early 1970s.

Connecting to Culture: Suggestions for Writing (p. 572)

The writing assignments that conclude the chapter offer students an opportunity to synthesize the ideas they've encountered in the readings and to make some conclusions about the assumptions outlined in the chapter introduction.

Constructing Nature: Evaluating Representations of Nature in Art

This project asks students to apply insights from their reading to a formal analysis of a work of art, whether music, fine art, photography, or film. Their papers should be founded on detailed observation, a careful critique of what they find, and a thoughtful consideration of how assumptions about nature inform cultural representations of the environment. They may want to enhance their analyses by researching the contexts in which a piece was produced or by locating any statements artists or critics may have made about the work. Although students may refer to Lopez, Ackerman, or other writers in the chapter, most important is that they form an interpretation based on their observations and support their analyses with details.

What Makes Tomatoes Juicy? Investigating the Food Industry

Combining field and library research, this assignment asks students to investigate how "natural" foods are produced and distributed to the market while it prompts them to question their own assumptions about what they eat. Eric Schlosser's essay offers a useful model for the kinds of information they might look for as well as how they might present their findings. Encourage them to skim through the rest of *Fast Food Nation* for additional information and sources. Note that reliable information about a food's origins, modifications, and suppliers can be difficult to obtain. Students might start their primary research by interviewing a grocery store's produce, dairy, or meat manager or buyer, who may be able to offer leads, and local advocacy groups might also be able to point them to good sources of information. If there is a food-processing or distribution facility nearby, suggest that your students arrange a tour and ask lots of questions when they visit. You may also want to direct students to the websites pre-pared by industry organizations for the benefit of their members. The U.S. Dairy Export Council, for example, offers a searchable directory of suppliers at usdec.org/Suppliers/index.cfm.

How to Connect to Nature: Proposing a Nature Trail

This project builds on Wangari Maathai's principle that nature can be both pre-served and used as a catalyst for social, cultural, and political change (see "Trees for Democracy," p. 501). As a starting point for their efforts, then, students might want to conduct some research on the uses and origins of nature trails to better understand their role in a community. The Rails-to-Trails Conservancy, for exam-ple, has written that "nature trails promote a sense of community . . . encourage outdoor activity and fitness, and . . . serve as historic and wildlife conservation areas," suggesting that nature trails are meant to do more than offer a navigable path through the woods. Students should attempt to articulate what existing trails' purposes (environmental, social, cultural, economic, and so on) are before they attempt to imagine a nature trail of their own. As they gather their infor-mation and write down their ideas, remind students that audience analysis is the key to a successful proposal. Even the best conceived trail will never see fruition if the designers cannot convince the decision makers of its worth.

Interrogating Assumptions: What's So Natural about Nature?

This final assignment calls for a text-based comparative analysis that synthesizes ideas from the chapter by evaluating several individual readings. To ensure coherence, encourage students to select readings that are closely related themat-ically as well as in the way they address assumptions about nature. If you've assigned any of the Interrogating Assumptions or Connecting to Another Reading questions that follow some of the readings in the chapter, allow your students to use their responses as starting points for their drafts. A successful student essay will posit a thesis about one of the assumptions and use the read-ings to support it, rather than simply compare and contrast several selections.

7 Technology

...or, what's so great about progress?

Even the simplest technologies can profoundly transform a culture. Consider the stirrup. When the Mongols added this small hoop of iron to saddles in the eleventh century, they transformed the horse from an agricultural tool and mode of transportation to a powerful instrument of war. The technology made it possible for the Mongols to stand as they rode, increasing their mobility and improving the accuracy of their aim. It gave them an advantage that many historians credit with allowing Genghis Khan to establish the most far-reaching empire of his day. Often taken for granted once they've been adopted, technologies—whether objects, skills, or organizations—have the power to change not only what people do, but also how they think. As students read the essays and respond to the assignments in this chapter, they will investigate how technology affects culture and vice versa. Becoming more conscious of technology's influences will help students become more critical technology users and consumers.

Issues of technology and nature are closely intertwined, so with that in mind, you may find it effective to teach this chapter in conjunction with the nature chapter that precedes it. Several of the readings in chapter 6 (especially those by Carl Elliott, Christine Rosen, Lewis Thomas, Susan McCarthy, and Eric Schlosser) touch on the themes explored in this chapter, and several of the readings in this chapter (including those by Thomas Hine, the *Onion*, Atul Gawande, and Daniel Harris) will augment students' understanding of the issues surrounding nature. The assignments in the two chapters complement each other nicely; in many cases, you might encourage students to use responses to questions in chapter 6 as starting points for their writing about technology, or vice versa.

Probably the biggest obstacle to exploring technology in a cultural-studies or composition class is overcoming student perceptions that something has to be a mechanical or electronic gadget to qualify as a technology (see assumption 1). The Examining the Everyday assignment that opens the chapter attempts to broaden definitions by prompting students to identify a physical technology that has nothing to do with electricity. Before you have your class attempt the assignment, you might consider exploring what "technology" is. Offer a tentative definition of "technology" as a tool, then, using the classroom environment as a starting point, work with your students to name everyday objects—such as the blackboard, chalk, books, spiral-bound notepads, perforated pages, window shades—that might qualify as technologies, and discuss how these objects affect the way they learn.

Because the central assumptions outlined in the chapter's introduction form the basis for analyzing the chapter's readings, spend some time discussing them in class. Use the questions that follow each discussion of an assumption to explore the concept with your students. You might want to ask your students whether they agree or disagree with the outlined assumptions, and what other assumptions about technology they can identify. Discuss with your class, also, how these assumptions function in American culture: Who holds them? What purposes do they serve? Are they helpful or harmful? And how do students see them played out in their personal lives and in the world around them?

All of the readings in this chapter question one or several of the three main assumptions outlined in the introduction: technologies are machines; technologies bring either progress or peril; and technologies are neutral. Langdon Winner's careful distinction between technological determinism and technological somnambulism provides a theoretical foundation for considering many of the questions raised by other readings. Several writers challenge machine-oriented definitions of technology: Ellen DeGeneres offers a wickedly funny take on the cultural drawbacks of new-and-improved products, Neil Postman argues that language is a human tool that shapes consciousness, and Malcolm Gladwell reports on the technological marvel of disposable diapers. The *Onion* satirizes our contemporary culture's obsession with technological breakthroughs. More serious consideration of the progresses and perils of technology can be found in Ellen Ullman's "The Museum of Me" (p. 639), which warns of the dangers of Internet commerce; Atul Gawande's "The Learning Curve" (p. 654), which considers how medical-training practices may hurt patients; and the paired readings on blogs, which suggest that Web publishing not only affects how people express themselves, but also how they interact. Underscoring the values, biases, and cultural influences connected to technology, Thomas Hine explores "smart" clothing and furniture, Gustav Peebles exposes the economic bias inherent in automated-teller machines, Clarence Page questions the need for space exploration, and Daniel Harris explains why Americans try to keep their homes lemony fresh.

Additional Resources

Nonfiction

Jacques Ellul, *The Technological Society* (1967) Ellul finds technology to be fundamentally threatening to human society. Though some of his examples are outdated now, Ellul's understanding of technology as a development of "technique" has important political implications.

Cass Sunstein, *Republic.com* (2001)   While many people believe that the Internet broadens perspectives, Sunstein argues that it naturally moves toward extremism. To combat this tendency, he proposes a system of government-sponsored public-media outlets to represent moderate views.

Film

The Matrix (1999)   *The Matrix* concerns the disillusionment of the hero, Neo, who learns that reality as he knows it is actually the construction of a larger, more frightening system.

Ellen DeGeneres, **This Is How We Live** (p. 588)

Comedian Ellen DeGeneres's take on technological progress will almost certainly strike a chord with students, who will recognize her tales of frustration with everyday technologies. As amusing as it is, however, the essay also effectively touches on all three of the assumptions from the chapter introduction. Included in DeGeneres's list of technologies that are "hurting us," for example, are obviously nonmechanical objects like breath strips and toilet paper. She questions the assumption that technologies bring either progress or peril by revealing that every perceived advance has a cost that's been overlooked. Allowing no middle ground in her contention that technologies make people lazy while they complicate interpersonal relationships, she also implies repeatedly that inventors and manufacturers are up to no good: "These are angry, angry people," she says, belying the assumption that technologies are neutral.

DeGeneres herself is among those consumers who accept complicating technologies. You may want to point out to your students that even as she rails against the inconvenience of modern conveniences, she also uncritically accepts the value of the basic technologies (CDs, scissors, batteries, light bulbs, toilets, cars, and telephones, for instance). It's the new-and-improved versions that drive her crazy. You might want to ask, then, at what point a technological improvement loses its value. What underlying forces prompt a culture to continually seek improvements to its existing tools?

Interrogating Assumptions

Every example DeGeneres cites has both positive and negative aspects. She praises the cell phone, for example, as "one beautiful thing" that "technology has done . . . for us" before she launches into a criticism of its shortcomings, the ways people abuse it, and its interpersonal consequences. Although she enjoys technological progress, DeGeneres suggests that improvements can be taken only so far before benefits turn into drawbacks. Any given technology, then, promises both progress *and* peril, depending on whether people accept it and what they do with it.

Writing about Cultural Practices

As students consider topics to write about, remind them that technologies can be not only objects but also practices or social structures. Reassure them as well that although they're welcome to model their essays on "This Is How We Live," they need not go after laughs if the prospect of attempting humor makes them uncomfortable. More important is that students treat this assignment as a critical narrative, not simply an opportunity to voice a complaint. The point of the exercise is to get students questioning their own assumptions as they investigate the cultural impetuses behind, and consequences of, a technology they might otherwise have taken for granted. Analyzing a personal annoyance will put them in a critical frame of mind that will help them more profitably approach the other works in this chapter.

Additional Resources

Television

Seinfeld, "The Finale (Part 1)"   In this episode, which aired in 1998, Elaine's use of a cell phone and call waiting in her efforts to speak with a friend whose father is ill digs her deeper and deeper into social faux pas. Kramer videotapes a crime in progress while they all watch, rather than help—a social failure that gets them arrested.

Web

Boing Boing, http://boingboing.net/   This Internet "directory of wonderful things" focuses largely on gadgetry.

"What Is the Most Important Invention of the Last Two Thousand Years?" http://www.edge.org/documents/Invention.html#DysonF   John Brockman posed the question to some of the world's leading scientists and technological innovators. Over one hundred responses are posted on this site.

Langdon Winner, **Technological Somnambulism** (p. 594)

Because the philosophical concepts of technological determinism and technological somnambulism apply to most of the writing in this chapter, Winner's essay is important foundational reading for students if they are to fully appreciate the other ideas they will encounter and explore. Although the selection is brief, Winner's ideas are complex. It will be well worthwhile to spend some time in class ensuring that students grasp the essay's points and understand the writer's argument.

At heart, Winner advocates for a cultural understanding of technology that probes deeper than how things are made and how they are used. Most people, he notes, are unconscious of the subtle and profound ways that technologies shape perception, morality, and human interaction. He wants his readers not only to recognize these influences but also to question them and, where appropriate, resist them. This is the key distinction between determinism and somnambulism as Winner presents the concepts: Where determinists would argue that social and cultural changes brought on by new technologies are inevitable, somnambulists would counter that they're inevitable only to the extent that they're ignored.

Because Winner's examples are more than 20 years old, they might seem dated to your students, which in turn might reduce their power. To illustrate Winner's points more concretely, you may want to consider additional examples with your students. In the case of word processing, you might ask them to respond to an assignment in longhand rather than in computer-generated type. Those who learned to compose on a keyboard will be surprised to discover how much the technology has shaped their ability to express themselves. To press home how technological constraints shape perception, you might ask students to consider how an area they know as drivers changes if they travel the same route by bicycle or on foot. Most will recognize that the same landscape appears completely different and takes on new meaning when a person is freed from the active process of driving a car.

As they contemplate Winner's points, encourage your students to think of some currently emerging technologies that offer the opportunity to examine new patterns of thinking and behavior as they develop and to speculate how those new tools and processes might alter their users' perceptions and interactions.

Interrogating Assumptions

Winner believes that a long-standing perception of technologies as neutral tools has blinded people to the cultural and moral implications of technological change. By thinking of technologies only in terms of how they work or how they are used and by taking for granted that there is nothing more to them, we overlook their deeper cultural impacts. And those impacts, he notes, are profound. New tools affect not only how people accomplish tasks but also how they think and how they interact; each new development forces a culture to renegotiate its rules and codes of behavior, which in turn shape individuals' consciousness.

Writing about Cultural Practices

By deconstructing a particular portrayal of computers in the popular media, students will have the opportunity to answer Langdon Winner's call to action. The challenge of the assignment will not be in choosing a representation for analysis, as Americans are bombarded daily with promises and threats that stem from computer applications. Rather, the challenge is to look past assumptions that computers are neutral tools that can be used either for good or for evil and to consider instead concerns about how a specific application might alter consciousness or affect interpersonal and cultural relationships. For a model analysis of a computer advertisement, direct students to Ellen Ullman's analysis of Packard Bell's 1996 "Wouldn't You Rather Be at Home?" television spot on page 643 of *ReMix*.

To help them probe deeper, as Winner advocates, you might want to explore an example of your own choosing with the class, discussing what it reveals about cultural attitudes toward computer technology (fear, excitement, ambivalence, and so on), and examine how the producers of the technology manipulate those attitudes for their own purposes. An excellent choice would be Apple's famous *1984* ad, which introduced the personal computer to an unsuspecting public (and which Packard Bell implicitly referenced in its own campaign 12 years later). At the time the Macintosh was released, most Americans, whose experience of computers was limited to bureaucratic, government, and some workplace applications, did not yet assume that a home computer was necessary or even desirable. Apple used general fears of computers as the ad's central theme, turning them back on themselves to present the Macintosh as a tool of *liberation* from bureaucratic, government, and workplace oppression. The spot, which was wildly successful in 1984, would not be effective today because the cultural attitudes it played against no longer hold. Showing the ad in class and discussing how it reveals assumptions from two decades ago should help students think more critically about contemporary examples.

Additional Resources

Nonfiction

Nicols Fox, *Against the Machine: The Hidden Luddite Tradition in Literature, Art, and Individual Lives* (2002)   Fox argues that Luddites get a bad rap and traces the tradition of resistance to technology from Ned Ludd through the Romantics and transcendentalists to modern dissenters.

Web

Apple Computer's "1984" advertisement, http://www.uiowa.edu/~commstud/ adclass/1984_mac_ad.html   This University of Iowa site contains both video of the ad and a shot-by-shot description.

"Apple's *1984*: The Introduction of the Macintosh in the Cultural History of Computers," http://www.duke.edu/~tlove/mac.htm   Ted Friedman's paper, presented at the Society for the History of Technology Convention in 1997, analyzes the ad and asks whether Apple has followed up on the claims it made.

Thomas Hine, **Looking Alive** (p. 602)

The cultural critique that Thomas Hine offers in this *Atlantic Monthly* article underscores why Langdon Winner calls for a philosophy of technology (see "Technological Somnambulism," p. 594). As Hine points out, designers' primary role in the marketing of technology is to subtly nudge people beyond practical thoughts about how things work or how they can be used. Before a technology will be accepted by its potential users, designers must create a desire for it or at least make it palatable. Most of us, however, don't pay critical attention to how this happens and tend to conclude that new technologies—even those that, as Hine puts it, seem "a little bit creepy"—are inescapable.

Through most of the twentieth century, Hine reports, designers made people comfortable with new technologies by camouflaging their inner workings and emphasizing their applications. Widespread mechanistic metaphors, which few people have questioned and most have embraced uncritically, have rendered modern society remarkably accepting of mechanical invasions of the body. As the latest technologies become more organic in appearance and function, however, entirely different metaphors are necessary. Modern designers have responded by turning their focus to technologies' inner workings, de-emphasizing anxieties about their applications in the process (often, it's not clear to anybody, including the designers, what those applications might ultimately be). By comparing metaphors, Hine suggests, one can discover a seismic shift in the culture's desires. If, in the 1950s, Americans dreamt of overcoming the body's limitations by grafting on machinery, in the first decade of the twenty-first century it appears that they hope to normalize that machinery by grafting on the body.

As Hine points out, predicting the future is a tricky thing. Despite the grand claims made by contemporary designers, there's no guarantee that they will succeed in getting people to accept new technologies. Take advantage of the "Found" list of predictions for the future (p. 606 of the book) by asking students what it reveals about people's desires in the 1950s. Encourage them to compile a comparable list of contemporary predictions for the future (using both Hine's article and their own imaginations). What does their list reveal about cultural desires today?

Writing about Cultural Practices

As students begin contemplating this assignment, remind them that they're not limited in their investigation to electronics or machines. Their first inclinations will likely be to research a major, successful innovation like the ones suggested in the assignment: the Internet, microwave ovens, compact discs, or any household appliance. However, you may also encourage your students to narrow their focus by choosing a limited aspect of a major technology (Web cameras, for example, or recordable CDs).

Whatever their subjects, students will need to both research a twentieth-century invention and compare the rhetorical claims surrounding it to claims that are currently being made about "smart" technologies. In addition to covering the predictions that Hine reviews, they might want to track down some up-to-date references to these technologies, which have already advanced significantly since the 2001 publication of "Looking Alive."

Additional Resources

Nonfiction

Ellen Lupton, with Grace Jeffers, Jennifer Tobias, and Alicia Imperiale, *Skin: Surface and Substance in Contemporary Design* (2002)   This book, which accompanied an exhibit at the Cooper-Hewitt National Design Museum, explores the convergence of the natural and the artificial. The designers featured foreground surfaces as the site of connection between people and objects.

Film

Hemo the Magnificent (1957)   In this animated film, directed by Frank Capra, the main character takes a tour through the human circulatory system. The sights he encounters are illustrated by microscope photographs of blood vessels.

Web

Wearable Computing, http://www.media.mit.edu/wearables/   MIT's site on truly "personal" computers collects news about advances in wearable technology.

Malcolm Gladwell, Smaller: The Disposable Diaper and the Meaning of Progress (p. 609)

On one level, Gladwell's history of the modern diaper effectively counters the assumption (see p. 578) that technologies are machines. Most people (even parents of babies) give very little thought to disposable diapers, and few would think of them as technology, much less a model of technological "perfection." But as Gladwell reveals, those innocuous little packages of plastic and padding represent an astounding compilation of technological marvels, including space-age polymers and superabsorbent chemical flakes that even scientists don't fully understand.

More compelling, Gladwell reveals the economic impetus behind efforts to make diapers smaller. The innovations weren't, he suggests, sought primarily for the benefits of consumers but for the producers. Although parents with young children have certainly benefited from the convenience of smaller disposable diapers, the makers of Huggies, Pampers, and the like actually invested a substantial amount of money and research in superabsorbent materials and similar technologies so that they could reduce their costs (of warehousing and transporting, for example) and make their products more profitable.

Students may notice that Gladwell's homage to the disposable diaper as a perfect innovation disregards some significant drawbacks associated with the product's invention and metamorphosis. His analysis is based on the assumption, for example, that the creation of disposable diapers was itself an improvement without a cultural price. But as environmentalists and cloth-diaper services are quick to point out, the nation's landfills are clogged annually with billions of plastic diapers that are not fully biodegradable, as well as millions of tons of untreated human waste. There is a significant financial cost as well: A year's supply of disposable diapers runs more than $2,000. At the same time, Gladwell hints at, but dismisses, another negative side effect of shrinking diapers: As diaper manufacturers became more efficient, they needed fewer plants, which resulted in factory closings and lost jobs. "Here," Gladwell intones, "is a partial explanation for the great wave of corporate restructuring that swept across America in the late '80s and early '90s: Firms could downsize their workforce because they had downsized their products." Students may well be bothered that this doesn't seem to count as a drawback in the writer's analysis. You might want to encourage them, then, to debate the effectiveness of Gladwell's essay as a whole and to consider whether unacknowledged assumptions detract from his argument.

Interrogating Assumptions

Gladwell sees the disposable diaper as a perfect innovation because it is one of the very few in modern life that exemplify Moore's Law, or "the rare instance in which there is no trade-off between size and performance." In grappling with the assumption that technology brings either progress or peril, many have concluded that improvements are necessarily coupled with trade-offs. Gladwell praises diapers because, considering their size and performance only, he sees no such compromise in their development. They not only have grown increasingly smaller but also have become more effective at what they were designed to do. Notice, however, the string of developments as Gladwell outlines them. Each new innovation (superabsorbent pads, breathable liners, and so on) has spawned a new problem that required an additional layer of technology to solve. The diaper may now be "perfect," in his estimation, but there is still room for improvement.

Writing about Cultural Practices

This assignment encourages students to analyze an everyday technology in a way that goes one step further than Malcolm Gladwell's analysis of the disposable diaper. Students will use Gladwell's approach as a starting point for their own investigations. Encourage your students to follow Gladwell's lead and choose a mundane, everyday item to examine. For inspiration, they might take an inventory of the contents of a closet or pocket, or they might carefully examine four feet of shelf space in a local supermarket.

Additional Resources

Nonfiction

Charles Panati, *Extraordinary Origins of Everyday Things* (1989)   A catalog of the stories behind familiar products, Panati's book covers everything from rabbits' feet to vasectomies.

Henry Petroski, *The Evolution of Useful Things* (1994)   Petroski's investigation of everyday items provides insights into the larger mechanism of cultural production.

Web

Diapers! Disposable or Cotton? http://www.ecobaby.com/cloth.htm   The Ecobaby site presents an argument against disposable diapers.

"The Poop on Eco-Friendly Diapers," http://www.wired.com/news/technology/0,1282,63182,00.html   *Wired* magazine looks into the real advantages of disposable diapers that are supposed to be environmentally sound.

Gustav Peebles, **A Wicked Cheat** (p. 617)

As you begin discussion of Peebles's argument, you may need to review with your class Langdon Winner's three categories of technology described in the chapter introduction (see pp. 578–79). To get the most out of "A Wicked Cheat," students need to understand that banking institutions and the industry's standard practices are themselves technologies. The ATM slip that Peebles annotates provides a record of those practices, revealing the cultural economic biases that inform them. In breaking down its components and revealing the history behind them, Peebles strongly rejects the assumption that technologies are neutral and proposes that fees be abolished in the interest of maintaining a fair and just society.

It's probable that your students will latch on to Peebles's argument, recognizing their own experiences in many of his examples. It shouldn't take much prodding to extract additional examples from your class: high interest rates, punitive fees, and perks for customers who maintain high balances, to name just a few. On the other hand, some students may contend that if banking customers gave some thought to the technologies they're using, they might be inspired to adjust their own practices; in other words, it's not the banks' or the government's responsibility to enforce good money-management practices among banking customers. If this happens, press your students to consider the larger context of banking, especially in urban and low-income areas. Keeping the focus on automated-teller fees, for example, you might want to point out that staffed branches are exceedingly rare in inner-city neighborhoods like Chicago's South Side. Also, point out that most ATMs are owned by third-party companies and not by the banks themselves. One question worth exploring is: If ATMs save the banks money, why do they charge their customers a fee to use them? You might use this question, or one like it, to prompt a thorough examination of the biases that inform the modern American banking industry. With a little thought, students should be able to expand Peebles's analysis with additional considerations and insights of their own.

Writing about Cultural Practices

Inspired by Peebles's biting analysis in "A Wicked Cheat," as well as targets of questionable banking practices themselves, students will likely be eager to conduct the investigation called for in this assignment. To keep it manageable, however, consider instructing them to focus their analysis on a single banking product—such as credit cards, debit cards, student loans, checking, online banking, or Paypal accounts—that has been offered to them personally. Once they have chosen a product, they might also want to obtain marketing materials for the same product aimed at a different audience (such as their parents) to provide a comparative basis for their analysis.

Several of your students may already have fallen into the credit trap and have a personal stake in this topic. Personal revelations and anecdotes may be useful components of an analysis, but remind your students that their goal is to critically assess how banking practices reveal cultural assumptions and biases toward young people, not to complain about their own financial situations.

For a sample student paper on the topic of credit cards and college students, see Matt Watson's "Hooked on Credit Cards" in Diana Hacker, *The Bedford Handbook*, Seventh Edition (Boston: 2005).

Additional Resources

Nonfiction

David and Tom Gardner, *The Motley Fool You Have More than You Think: The Foolish Guide to Personal Finance* (2001)   The introduction and first chapter of this financial self-help book offer a scathing review of banking practices and cultural assumptions about money, especially as they relate to young people.

Fiction

Horatio Alger, *Ragged Dick* (1868)   In this rags-to-riches story about a New York City street boy, Alger considers the benefits for the poor of using a bank.

Banking with the Poor, http://www.bwtp.org/   The Banking with the Poor
  Network advocates poverty relief through finance reform.

Neil Postman, **Invisible Technologies** (p. 623)

Although his essay is brief and his language accessible, Postman's concept may
be challenging for your students. One way to ease students into Postman's point
of view is to explore any experiences they may have had with learning other languages. Be careful, however, not to focus on students who are bilingual by
upbringing. Asking them to speak on behalf of their communities or ethnicities
is culturally insensitive and politically dangerous. Turn, instead, to the educational experience. A majority of high schools, and most colleges and universities,
require students to study a second language, so it's likely that most, if not all, of
your students have spent at least some time attempting to learn one. A common
aspect of learning another language is that the effort tends to highlight elements
of English that native speakers take for granted. Difficulties in making straight
translations often reveal cultural differences as well, as Postman explains with
his example of Japanese language and the scientific method. Using that example as a starting point, ask your students to share similar revelations they may
have experienced with another language.

Interrogating Assumptions

Postman's examination of language as a technology is intended to discredit the
assumption that technologies can be neutral. Note that this excerpt is part of the
writer's introduction to a chapter that explores "invisible" technologies to reveal
how they influence human consciousness and cultural perspectives. To help students grapple with this idea, turn their attention back to the writer's initial definition of "ideology": "a set of assumptions of which we are barely conscious but
which nonetheless directs our efforts to give shape and coherence to the world"
(par. 1). Precisely because language is unconscious, it shapes its speakers' worldview in ways they often cannot recognize. Postman's goal is to make the invisible ideological processes of language visible.

Writing about Cultural Practices

This assignment asks students not to judge the biases and assumptions inherent in a given questionnaire, but rather to unearth them and consider how they
might affect a respondent's answers. If you have assigned any of the Writing
about Cultural Practices projects in *ReMix* that involved having students com-

pose and distribute a questionnaire, you might consider encouraging students to use their previous work as the subject of their analyses; it may be easier for them to identify the assumptions and purposes that informed their questions, and armed with Postman's critique, students may be surprised to discover how they might have structured their questionnaires differently. Otherwise, suggest that they look for a questionnaire that poses a combination of objective and subjective questions in several formats—multiple choice, fill-in-the-blank, and open-ended queries, for example—and consider why the writers structured some questions differently than they structured others. Note that in addition to the questionnaire sources suggested in the text, students might also consider magazine self-assessment quizzes, questionnaires designed to help people diagnose their own medical symptoms, job applications, marketing surveys, or a local or federal census form. (For a critical analysis of a single question on the U.S. Census, refer students to Russell Thornton's essay "What the Census Doesn't Count," p. 65.) You might even suggest that students analyze a set of questions that follow one of the readings in the textbook itself to uncover the author's efforts to direct their thinking.

Additional Resources

Nonfiction

John McWhorter, *The Power of Babel: A Natural History of Language* (2001)
McWhorter complicates the common notion of language development as a family tree. Charting instances of linguistic changes, he concludes that languages form a web of relationships.

Steven Pinker, *The Language Instinct: How the Mind Creates Language* (1994)
Addressing the nature/nurture debate over language acquisition, Pinker suggests that our ability to learn language depends on both biological and social factors.

Web

Esperanto.net, http://www.esperanto.net/   The home page of Esperanto explains why the creators set out to make an artificial language. The existence of constructed languages, of which Esperanto is the most famous, challenges the invisibility of linguistic functions.

Jill Walker, **Weblog: A Definition** (p. 628)
Bonnie A. Nardi, Diane J. Schiano, Michelle Gumbrecht, and Luke Swartz, **Why We Blog** (p. 629)

Blogging, which first became popular around 2002, taps into the Internet's potential as a communication medium. Most observers celebrate blogging's potential as an unfiltered publishing tool, and these writers are no exception. Students may notice that both articles explore blogging techniques and uses in largely positive terms but that neither delves into the cultural implications posed by this new technology. It would be interesting to examine them in the context of Neil Postman's essay on language (p. 623) and Langdon Winner's musings in "Technological Somnambulism" (p. 594): If language shapes consciousness, how might emerging communication technologies affect the ways people think and interact?

Although Jill Walker's definition of "weblog" will be useful for students unfamiliar with the phenomenon, and the sample blogs offer compelling examples, classroom discussion should probably center on the research findings presented in "Why We Blog." Nardi, Schiano, Gumbrecht, and Swartz focus on bloggers' motivations, not their cultural impact. In other words, they're interested in what bloggers expect to gain by using the technology. Their findings suggest that in the case of this application, at least, technologies tend to be adapted by individuals to meet their own needs, despite what uses its designers may have intended or expected. Although the authors do not consider the social and cultural consequences of the emerging popularity of blogs, encourage your students to discuss the implications of their research. You might choose one of the five motivations they catalog—blogs to "document my life," blogs as commentary, blogs as catharsis, blogs as muse, and blogs as community forum—and ask your students to examine the authors' examples in light of how that particular use affects both the bloggers' consciousness and their cultural positions. In the first instance, for example, the medium seems to relieve users of the need to maintain regular personal contact with individual members of their circle of family and friends, which may result in unanticipated isolation despite the constant updates. How might this technology change social interaction, both for better and for worse?

Writing about Cultural Practices

If you plan to assign the end-of-chapter blogging project (see p. 672), this initial analysis of an existing blog will prove very helpful in getting students to think about how blogs are structured, maintained, and received. Indeed, this assignment is a useful prompt for students' initial posts in their own blogs. They'll notice very quickly that central to most blogging is a keen awareness of audience—something that should be central to all forms of writing but is easily forgotten. In blogging forums, however, the audience can (and often does) respond, which makes the medium something of a cross between written and oral communication.

Responses should consist of a close reading of one writer's blog, rather than a general overview of a host site like blogger.com or TypePad. In addition to using the bulleted questions as a guide for describing what they find in some detail, students might consider how the three assumptions about technology outlined in the chapter introduction inform both bloggers' efforts and their own interpretations. They may also want to continue the classroom discussion by questioning how the medium may influence the writer's consciousness and how the blog of their choosing adapts to or promotes new ways of communicating with others.

Additional Resources

Fiction

Jessica Cutler, *The Washingtonienne* (2005)   This fictionalized adaptation of Cutler's prurient blog relates the details of her affair with a congressman. Because it was one of the first published books to come out of a popular blog, many reviewers took notice of the book as part of a potential trend.

Web

Bloggercon, http://www.bloggercon.org/   Bloggercon brought bloggers together in the real world. On this site, you can read about how organizers structured the meetings to follow the conventions of blogging rather than those of standard conference panels.

Andrew Sullivan, "The Blogging Revolution: Weblogs Are to Words What Napster Was to Music," http://www.wired.com/wired/archive/10.05/mustread.html?pg=2   One of the most widely read bloggers describes how he decided to begin publishing online.

Ellen Ullman, **The Museum of Me** (p. 639)

Ullman's critique of the Internet offers a clear example of the progress-or-peril assumption that tends to permeate ideas about technology. Drawing on her extensive industry expertise—she was one of the first computer programmers in the 1970s—to prove her claim, she warns that the current incarnation of the Internet threatens to redefine social relationships and to "affect the very structure of reality." By creating "the actual infrastructure of an individualized marketplace," she believes, the Internet is producing a society that devalues community. Far from being a positive technology, she argues, the Internet is no longer asocial but increasingly antisocial. The end result, she intones, will be a wider gulf between economic classes, personal isolation, the death of democracy, and a world without culture—all in the name of higher profit margins for the companies that provide goods and services.

Ullman explicitly rejects assumptions that the Internet is neutral. Rather, she argues that designers and programmers are actively and deliberately cutting people off from social interaction with other human beings. Although Americans are being taught that the process of removing facilitators from economic transactions, or "disintermediation," is a form of progress that increases freedom and opportunities, Ullman argues the opposite. As she sees it, recent changes in the ways people perceive and use the Internet are the result of deliberate efforts to restructure capitalism for the benefit of the wealthy. The goal, she suggests, is to eliminate jobs, especially those that the disadvantaged have historically pursued as a means of entry into the middle class. The middle classes, too, face a future in which they no longer have access to services and must do everything themselves. Students may notice that Ullman's concerns echo Langdon Winner's warnings about technological somnambulism (see p. 594): A profound change is taking place, yet nobody seems to notice.

If Ullman's position seems extreme to your students, use their resistance to encourage thoughtful analyses of their own. How would they counter her argument?

Writing about Cultural Practices

Although the Internet is a relatively recent technology, most people with access have said at some point or another that they can't imagine how they ever got along without it. This assignment encourages students to probe this almost universal sentiment to uncover how dependence on the Internet affects the ways people live. There is some risk that informants will self-censor their online activities as your students watch, knowing both that they're being observed and that they will be the subjects of an academic paper. Rather than observing in real time, then, students might consider asking their informants to keep logs of their time online or simply to share an hour's worth of history from their toolbars. More fruitful for the assignment might be the interview portion, which lets students ask their informants directly about how they use the Internet and what that usage means to them. Stress that students should prepare interview questions before they meet; you might want to work with the class to compile a list of questions they may draw on.

Before they begin their field research, encourage students to review the essay "Why We Blog" (p. 629), which outlines the research methodology used for a professional report on a related topic. Because the authors are careful to explain who they chose to study, how they studied them, and what their goals were, their paper may help students think about the best ways to structure their own research, as well as serve as a model for their own writing.

Additional Resources

Web

"Deconstructing a Mass Media Image of the Library," http://library.otis.edu/drearylib.htm   This Otis College of Art and Design site presents still images from the Packard Bell "Wouldn't You Rather Be at Home?" television spot and an analysis of how the company aligns libraries with oppression.

"Ghosts in the Machines," http://www.citypaper.com/news/story.asp?id=8182 In this feature from the Baltimore *City Paper,* Ryan Boddy considers a complication of the elaborate online lives people construct: What happens when someone dies?

"Who Says the Net Makes Cities Obsolete?" http://archive.salon.com/aug97/21st/cities970807.html   In an essay from 1997, Thomas J. Campanella argues that Internet webcams can reinforce the physicality of the city.

The Onion, New Technological Breakthrough to Fix Problems of Previous Breakthrough (p. 647)

In typical *Onion* fashion, the writers of this article use irreverent humor to raise a serious question: If technological breakthroughs can cause as much harm as good, why does modern culture embrace scientific research unequivocally? In essence, they're taking a dig at the cultural biases that support research—the uncritical belief, for example, that anything based in science must be good and that new is always better. As the satire hints, scientists themselves work hard to perpetuate these beliefs. Mock quotations throughout the piece imply that scientists never acknowledge failure, nor does the press. A technological disaster is, instead, repositioned as an opportunity to explore technological solutions.

Students may not be accustomed to questioning the progress model of modern history; it is so deeply ingrained in contemporary thinking that it seems natural. You might need to explain that until the scientific revolution of the eighteenth century, most people viewed any kind of change as a dangerous threat, resisting ideas of "improvement" and looking backward to an imagined idyllic past. Enlightenment writers and thinkers, entranced with the new idea of "reason" and excited by the discoveries of the period, began to argue that every change represented progress toward an imagined idyllic future. Science itself, then, is largely responsible for the current assumption that scientific advances should be pursued at any cost.

Those costs, however, can be high. As the *Onion* story suggests, scientific advances can have unintended, and even disastrous, consequences. Worse, those consequences can snowball, creating new problems much more serious than the original ones had been. Work through the article with your students to outline the fictional cycles of improvement and harm it chronicles and ask them to brainstorm some real-world parallels. Can they think of any scientific break-throughs that caused problems that had to be solved with additional scientific breakthroughs? For some examples from the book, you might refer them to Lewis Thomas's "On Cloning a Human Being" (p. 532), Susan McCarthy's "On Immortality" (p. 544), Eric Schlosser's "Why McDonald's Fries Taste So Good" (p. 552), Ellen DeGeneres's "This Is How We Live" (p. 588), Malcolm Gladwell's "Smaller: The Disposable Diaper and the Meaning of Progress" (p. 609), Atul Gawande's "The Learning Curve" (p. 654), and Daniel Harris's "Cleanness" (p. 661).

Writing about Cultural Practices

Certainly, scientific advances often improve human life. However, when we focus only on the benefits, we may overlook potential hazards and unanticipated consequences. Sometimes those consequences can change or structure our lives in ways that are not always desirable or intended. And sometimes technologies do not fulfill all of the needs we hope they will. This writing assignment encourages students to consider these issues as they apply to current events—specifically, to a controversial scientific project that is either being proposed or is already underway. Because they will be investigating a project that has triggered debate, students will almost certainly form their own opinions on the issue. Remind them that their purpose in this assignment is not to argue a position but to critically examine how a reporter, an editor, or a columnist has explained a project or argued his or her own position.

Note, too, that the type of writing students choose to examine will influence the direction of their analyses. Editorials and columns explicitly argue a position, but articles are supposed to be objective. The former, then, will be easier to evaluate, but locating the hidden biases of the latter may prove more interesting.

Additional Resources

Nonfiction

Gregg Easterbrook, *The Paradox of Progress: How Life Gets Better while People Feel Worse* (2003)   Easterbrook believes that progress really has made things easier—people are wealthier, the environment is cleaner, crime and disease are declining—but not many people know it.

The Onion, Our Dumb Century (1999)   The *Onion* doesn't just satirize recent progress. In their recap of the past 100 years, the *Onion* writers take on industrialization, automobiles, and space travel.

Engineering Disasters and Learning from Failure, http://www.matscieng
.sunysb.edu/disaster/ This SUNY Stonybrook site surveys some of the
most catastrophic engineering failures of recent times and explores the
ethics of learning from mistakes.

Clarence Page, **Should We Still Be Involved in Space Exploration?** (p. 650)

In a compelling but unpopular argument, Clarence Page calls on his readers, as
well as Congress and NASA, to reexamine the assumptions that underlie the
ongoing support of the U.S. space program. As Page points out, the U.S. government originally determined to send men into space not out of scientific
curiosity, but out of political imperative. The sole purpose was to get there before
the Russians did. By reminding his readers that the space program is a remnant
of the cold war, Page underscores the point that technology is anything but neutral. This op-ed piece questions not only whether it's still necessary (or wise) to
send human beings into space but also whether previous missions have accomplished enough to justify the risks.

Students may notice that although he alludes to them, Page deliberately
refrains from cataloging the many scientific achievements with which NASA is
credited. Space proponents frequently respond to criticisms like Page's by pointing out that NASA's research has resulted in several technological advances that
have been successfully applied in fields as varied as medicine, transportation,
consumer electronics, textiles, and computers. Page argues, however, that those
achievements do not explain Americans' fascination with space exploration. The
reason for widespread support of the space program, he suggests, is emotional.
America loves NASA because it represents the future and the *idea* of progress, if
not progress itself.

Interrogating Assumptions

Although many Americans think of the space program and its accomplishments
as the epitome of progress, Page reminds his readers that NASA has seen its
share of disasters. Although the political reasons behind manned expeditions
ceased to apply when the cold war ended, American astronauts are still dying in
fiery crashes. And despite the staggering amount of time and resources that have
been devoted to manned shuttle flights, the space program relies on seriously
outdated technologies. The progress popularly ascribed to space exploration,
Page implies, is illusory at best.

Writing about Cultural Practices

This critical assignment asks students to consider how assumptions surrounding technology color American attitudes toward space exploration. By viewing and analyzing a film or television show in which space travel figures prominently, students have the opportunity to answer Clarence Page's implied question: *Why* do Americans remain so enamored of the space program? Technological advancements aside, what have we gained from it, and what do we expect to gain in the future?

Although they need only write about a single movie or television program, encourage your students to view several examples of the genre before they select the focus for their papers. They will likely notice similar themes, conflicts, and plotlines through many of them, which should prompt them to question what those themes reveal. Because Clarence Page emphasizes the cold-war politics behind the founding of the space program, you might also want to consider requiring your students to examine at least one movie or show from the cold-war era and one produced in the 1990s or later, looking for evidence of how shifting cultural contexts affect the story's themes. The *Alien* films, which span 22 years, are especially revealing.

Following is a brief list of movies and television shows that might work for this assignment.

Movies

Apollo 13 (1995)	*Galaxy Quest* (1999)
Alien (1975)	*Hitchhiker's Guide to the Galaxy* (2004)
Aliens (1986)	*The Martian Chronicles* (1980)
Alien³ (1992)	*The Right Stuff* (1983)
Alien: Resurrection (1997)	*Solaris* (2002)
Contact (1997)	*Space Cowboys* (2000)
Destination Moon (1950)	*Starship Troopers* (1997)
Explorers (1985)	Any *Star Trek* movie
Flash Gordon (1980)	*2001: A Space Odyssey* (1968)
Forbidden Planet (1956)	

Television

Battlestar Galactica (1978–1979, 2004–)

Buck Rogers in the Twenty-fifth Century (1979–1981)

Lost in Space (1965–1968)

Red Dwarf (British, 1988)

Space 1999 (1975–1977)

Stargate: SG1 (1997–)

Any *Star Trek* series

Atul Gawande, **The Learning Curve** (p. 654)

Students may not realize at first that Gawande's essay is part of a larger debate about medical practices and regulations. As deadly hospital errors become increasingly publicized, several policy makers have lobbied for legislation that would require that patients be informed of a doctor's level of experience before a procedure is performed, giving them the opportunity to demand treatment from a more practiced physician. Gawande, whose professional research interests focus on issues of medical error, has countered in several articles that although such concerns are valid, the proposed system of informed consent would seriously hamper the profession's ability to train new doctors, thus causing more patients harm in the long run.

This essay (published in a slightly different version in *Complications* under the title "Education of a Knife") makes that point through confessional narrative. Gawande describes in minute and sometimes gruesome detail how he learned a "simple" medical procedure. He notes that as a student of a procedure he was acutely aware of every element involved, but nonetheless "bumbled" his way through it. Only after several botched attempts did he finally master the process. This, he stresses, is the case for every new doctor. None of the skills required for successful medicine come naturally. They are, instead, learned through a halting and repeated series of instruction, trial, and error.

One of Gawande's primary reasons for writing is to make people understand that despite the authority patients confer on medical practitioners, doctors are not infallible. Many complicated procedures are uncertainly performed by amateurs every day. Even experienced physicians must learn new skills without formal training, and they make mistakes. Central to the success of Gawande's argument is his humility: In honestly describing his own mistakes, Gawande breaks down the traditional barrier between doctor and patient, inviting his readers to put themselves in a medical student's position to better understand how the medical field works. His goal is not to alarm people or to suggest that they refuse treatment from medical students, but to disabuse the public of the growing notion that doctors can perfect their skills without putting at least some of their patients at risk. If patients had the opportunity to refuse being practiced on, he suggests, doctors—new and experienced alike—would never learn.

Interrogating Assumptions

"The Learning Curve" describes several facets of medicine that belie the notion that technology is a machine. Using the essay as a guide, work with your students to identify the myriad forms of technology that are essential to modern medicine. In addition to learning how to use tools and machines, for example, doctors must master individual procedures, each of which has been fine-tuned over many years and adapted as new technologies become available. Relationships—doctor/resident, doctor/patient, resident/patient—are themselves learned systems. Even communication is highly structured. Surgeons must learn what to say to patients, what not to say, what body language to use. You might want to create a column on the board for each of Langdon Winner's three categories of technology (see pp. 578–79 in this chapter's introduction)— apparatuses, skills and techniques, social organizations—and list Gawande's examples where they fit.

Writing about Cultural Practices

Asking students to reflect on their own learning processes will help them to become more active learners. Before they begin drafting their personal narratives of learning episodes, consider spending some time discussing what contributes to the effectiveness of the essay on which they will be modeling their own work. They may note, for example, how Gawande combines objective detail with personal reflection or that his honesty and humility incline readers to like him and be open to his point of view.

Students' first inclination as they approach their papers may be to write about learning something major and complicated, such as driving, speaking a foreign language, or skiing. Large subjects, however, will likely prove too complex to analyze well in just a few pages. Encourage your students to focus on a single aspect of their new environment or skill, much as Gawande focuses on the discrete practice of inserting a central line to make a larger point about medical training. Remind them, as well, that they need not focus on traditional mechanical skills. "Soft" skills like interpersonal communications, navigating office politics, time management, or familiarity with specialized jargon would be effective topics for this assignment.

Finally, be sure students understand that their purpose is not to teach a skill to their readers but to critically assess how learning a specific task affected their sense of who they are. In addition to describing a process, then, they should also be careful to consider its personal and cultural implications.

Additional Resources

Nonfiction

Perri Klass, *A Not Entirely Benign Procedure: Four Years as a Medical Student* (1987)   In these essays, reprinted from the *New York Times,* Klass describes her time at Harvard Medical School, including the difficulty of conflict between medical objectivity and compassion.

Television

ER, "Do One, Teach One, Kill One"   In this episode from 1995, Carter loses his first patient due to a surgical error.

Web

Belleview Literary Review, http://www.blreview.org/   A publication of the NYU Department of Medicine, *Belleview* focuses on writing that explores illness or healing. You can read selections from previous issues in the archive.

Daniel Harris, **Cleanness** (p. 661)

To improve your chances of a productive discussion session of Harris's complex observations and writing style, consider assigning students the task of outlining or paraphrasing his major points as they read his essay, and tell them to be prepared to discuss his arguments when they come to class.

In essence, "Cleanness" deconstructs the rhetorical and ethical dimensions of modern cleaning imagery to argue that advertising has raised contemporary standards of cleanliness to extreme heights in a conscious effort to "enslav[e] us to products." He breaks this discourse into five parts: (1) the aesthetic of cleanliness; (2) the demonization of bacteria; (3) the objectification of the human body combined with the sensualization of objects; (4) the obsession with shiny surfaces; and (5) the juxtaposition of militarism with femininity. To help focus discussion, you might want to select, or ask your students to select, the aspect you or they find most interesting and focus on what Harris has to say about it.

Interrogating Assumptions

As "Cleanness" suggests, the value of most new technologies is not immediately apparent to consumers. Technologies, in other words, have to be sold. Rather than assume that consumers will embrace the benefits of, and rush to buy, every new product that comes along, manufacturers and advertisers work together to create desire for their technologies. In the case of cleaning products, Harris argues, this has been accomplished largely by convincing people that unseen dangers lurk in every corner and that artificial smells offer the only acceptable evidence that those threats have been obliterated. Rather than neutral tools for eliminating visible and tangible dirt, cleaning products have contributed to a cultural redefinition of what constitutes filth in the first place.

Writing about Cultural Practices

Although most students will consider themselves savvy consumers of marketing messages, tell them you expect them to focus on details from the images themselves and to question every aspect of a given advertisement, from the images to the text to the cultural context. To help focus their analyses, students should consider examining the ads in the context of Harris's arguments. They might, for example, consider militaristic imagery in ads for household cleaners, the presentation of artificial scents, animated manifestations of otherwise invisible threats, the feminization of cleaning tasks, or comparisons between human and technological objects. Students should also be careful to consider the audience for the advertisements they choose to examine, questioning how the gender, age, and class status of the target market affects how the advertisers portray their products.

To help students get a feel for the kind of analysis this project calls for, you might want to apply its questions as a class to the images in the Sampling the Old and the New feature on pages 600–1 of the book. The ads for washing machines, one from 1874 and one from 2005, offer excellent illustrations of several of Harris's points and will give students the opportunity to practice evaluating how cleanliness is marketed without feeling the pressure of writing for a grade.

Additional Resources

Nonfiction

Susan Strasser, *Never Done: A History of American Housework* (1982)   In her study of the housewife's "separate sphere," Strasser analyzes how technological advances in cleaning changed women's lives.

Web

"Laboring Under a Disinfectant," http://www.mindfully.org/Health/Disinfectant-Obsession-Misguided.htm   In this article, originally from the *New York Times*, scientists question whether the American war against bacteria does more harm than good.

The Vintage Vacuum Cleaner Museum, http://www.137.com/museum/ This brief history of the development and sale of vacuum cleaners contains several early advertising images.

Mixing Words and Images:
Annotating a Technological Object (p. 671)

As part of a culture, technologies are inherently imbued with the values and biases of their designers. Technologies are not neutral. This does not imply that the values underlying a technology are harmful—just that they should not be taken for granted. This assignment encourages students to look beyond the surface applications of an everyday technology (its usefulness, as it were) and to tease out the biases and values from which it emerged.

If your students completed the Examining the Everyday assignment that opens the chapter, encourage them to annotate the same objects they chose before they worked through the readings. Most will discover that they have different ideas about those items and will delight in exploring their newly complicated understandings. They should feel free, as well, to incorporate any of the phrases or paragraphs they wrote initially, although most will discover that their earlier work is no longer adequate enough to express their thoughts.

Harper's Magazine publishes annotations similar to Gustav Peebles's "A Wicked Cheat" (p. 617) on a regular basis. To help your students become more comfortable with this type of writing, as well as to spark ideas for an object worth annotating, encourage them to go to the library and examine several examples from the magazine's back issues. They can also sometimes find annotations at the *Harper's* website, harpers.org, under "Features," but the layout makes them difficult to read in electronic format.

Although students are not writing a traditional research paper, research is a necessary component of this assignment. It will not be enough for students simply to make observations or to speculate about a technology's possible underlying biases. To compose a thoughtful analysis, they will need to learn the object's (or practice's) history and draw conclusions about what they discover. To stress the importance of research, you might require that students submit a bibliography that lists the sources they consulted. Finally, as they prepare their annotations, remind students that although they are not writing a traditional essay, their individual points should—like Peebles's—relate to each other and work together to form a coherent argument.

Connecting to Culture: Suggestions for Writing (p. 672)

The writing assignments that conclude the chapter offer students an opportunity to synthesize the ideas they've encountered in the readings and to make some conclusions about the assumptions outlined in the chapter introduction.

Why Context Matters: Investigating Technology Use

This field-research assignment asks students to apply the chapter's three assumptions to a close observation of how cultural context affects the uses and influences of technology. Students should start by identifying the group they want to observe. Although they might be interested in writing about a group to which they belong, you may also suggest that they consider a community that they are not a part of. In addition to observing from a distance, encourage your students to interview several members of the group they choose to examine. They might ask their informants to offer their own answers to the questions posed in the assignment and compare those answers to what they observed.

Each student's paper should include a narrative section that describes in detail his or her chosen group's physical setting, specific interactions, and several examples of how it uses specific technologies. The next part of their paper should analyze how both the group and the individual members adapt technologies for their own purposes, considering the three assumptions about technology around which the chapter is structured.

Interrogating Assumptions: Blogging as a Form of Critical Analysis

Although this twist on keeping a course journal is presented as a chapter-concluding project, it will work best if you assign it up front when you start exploring the readings with your students. If you do have a class weblog set up and want to have your students take on this experiment, assign the paired readings on blogs ("Weblog: A Definition," p. 628, and "Why We Blog," p. 629) either very early in the sequence or at the end, depending on how much metacognition you want to foster. The project will be most effective if, in addition to having students keep their own blogs, you require them to read and respond to their classmates' entries as well.

Tracing the Internet: Using the Wayback Machine

This project asks students to examine multiple versions of one website in an effort to analyze how the Internet has evolved. Although certainly not necessary, reading Ellen Ullman's critical overview of changes to the Internet may help students think about the Web as a site of cultural transformation. Changes to websites not only underscore the simple fact that technologies are constantly evolving but also reveal how the nature, purpose, and application of this technology has adapted to the cultural changes the Internet itself has wrought. Be aware that the Wayback Machine is an amazing tool; it's easy to get absorbed in it and lose track of time. If students have completed any of the book's several Writing about Cultural Practices assignments that ask them to visit a website, they might want to start their investigation with a site they've already written about. Note, too, that if students choose a major organization's site for their investigation, they may find themselves overwhelmed by the sheer number of pages contained within it. To keep the project manageable, students might want to focus their analysis on a single page or small group of pages within a major site; you might also want to give them the option of focusing on a less extensive site that has been around for several years.